TOGETHER IN STRUGGLE

TOGETHER IN STRUGGLE

India and Indonesia 1945-1949

V. Suryanarayan

PRABHAT PRAKASHAN
prabhatbooks@gmail.com

Antar Rashtriya Sahayog Parishad
arspindia@gmail.com

Published by
PRABHAT PRAKASHAN
4/19 Asaf Ali Road,
New Delhi-110 002 (INDIA)
Tele : +91-11-23289777
e-mail: prabhatbooks@gmail.com

ISBN 978-93-5266-666-9
TOGETHER IN STRUGGLE
by V. Suryanarayan

Edition
First, 2018

Price
₹ 300.00 (Rupees Three Hundred only)

Printed at
R-Tech Offset Printers, Delhi

To
P.R.S. Mani
who
kindled my interest in
Indonesian Revolution

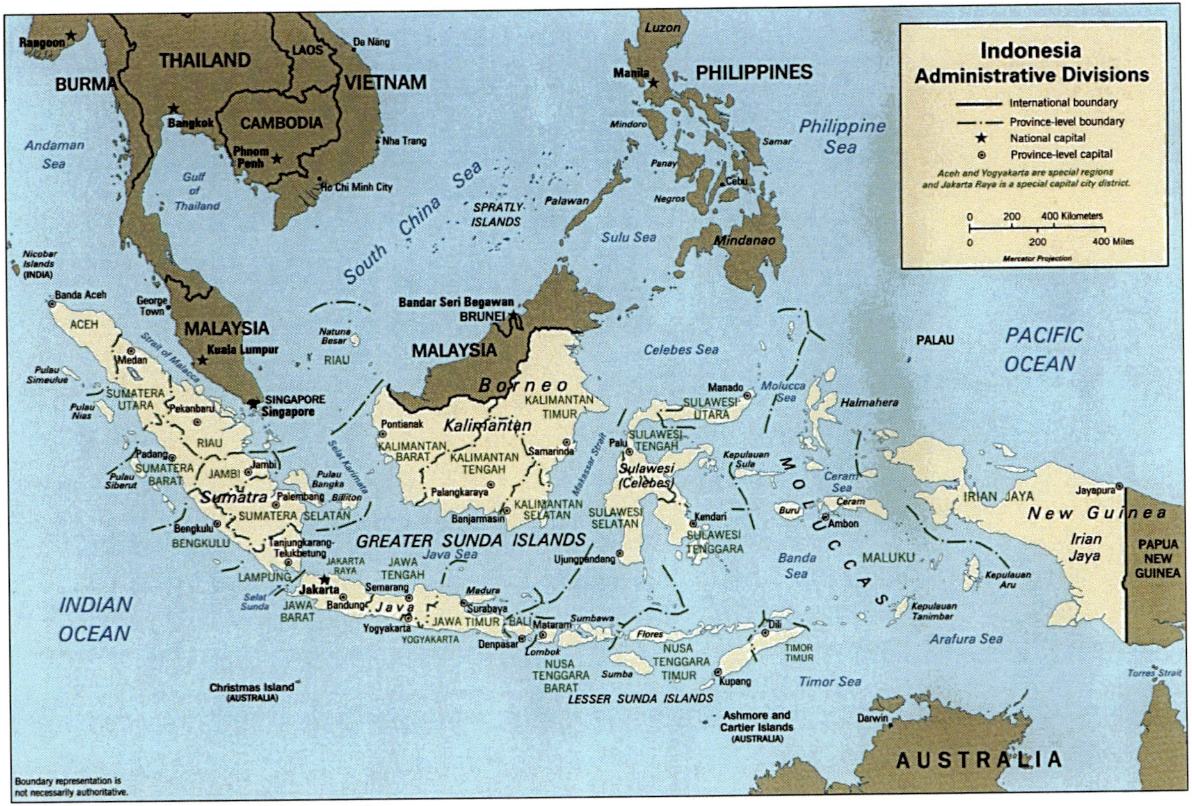

Courtesy: Government of Indonesia

Foreword

For centuries, India and Indonesia have been linked by winds that blow across the Indian Ocean. From Tamralipti in Bengal to Bharuch in Gujarat, the coastal regions had fruitful links with Indonesia. In Odisha, every year, on the full moon day in the month of Karthik (Karthik Poornima), people place lamps in small boats, made out of banana stems or corks, and float them in ponds, rivers and the sea. Known as Bali Yatra, the festival symbolizes the voyage through the sea, in ancient times, which linked Kalinga with the distant Bali. Even today the people of Indian origin, who live in Southeast Asia, are referred to as Klings.

There are other striking similarities between India and Indonesia. While drafting the Constitution, the founding fathers of Indonesia, the country with the largest Muslim population in the world, decided not to make Indonesia an Islamic state, but resolved to make it secular. They were determined not to follow the policy of cultural straight jacketing. They recognized both linkages and diversities; therefore, the national motto of Indonesia is Bhinneka Tunggal Eka, meaning though diverse we are one. Similarities with India are obvious.

The Indonesian leaders are extremely proud of their Hindu cultural heritage. Throughout Indonesia, especially in Java, there are innumerable monuments which glorify their Hindu moorings. I would like to mention an interesting incident in this connection. In the late 1950's, Pakistan was trying to build friendship with Indonesia on the basis of Islamic solidarity. But Sukarno rebuffed the idea and told Z. A. Bhutto, "We are Muslims by faith, but Hindus by cultural heritage".

Indian cultural imprint in Indonesia is clearly visible. Indianised kingdoms like Sri Vijaya, Mataram, Sailendra, Singhosari and Majapahit, the Agastya cult in Java, familiar Sanskrit words in Bahasa Indonesia; architectural monuments like Borobudur and Lara Djonggrang, literary masterpieces like Amaramala, Arjuna Vijaya and Bharata Yuddha, the Wayang Kulit based on the Ramayana and Mahabharata themes, living Indian cultural traditions in the island of Bali – all these are testimony to the courage and zeal of Indian princes, poets, priests, artisans and merchants and the assimilable qualities of the Indonesian people.

This book is devoted to the study of India-Indonesia relations during 1945–1949 when the two countries were friends engaged in similar struggle. During Indonesia's struggle for independence, India was its closest ally. The nationalist triumvirate–Sukarno, Mohammad Hatta and Sutan Sjahrir– have frequently acknowledged their cultural and political indebtedness to India. As Sukarno has written, "India and Gandhi frequently inspired me and, during those years which I spent in prison, it was my strong belief in God and the inspiring spirit of India that raised my hopes and my own faith in our cause".

I congratulate Prof. V. Suryanarayan heartily, for writing an excellent book on an important phase of India-Indonesia relations. He has consulted a wide variety of primary and secondary sources to give it a sound research base. Lucidly written, the book provides refreshing insights. It should be of interest to all those who want to foster and promote India-Indonesia relations.

Indonesia is our closest maritime neighbour. But unfortunately, for a variety of reasons, we remain intellectually distant. In the present context when India is poised to convert Look East policy into Act East policy, this book will definitely provide an excellent reference material and above all give a deep insight into India-Indonesia relations.

(Vinay Sahasrabuddhe)
President,
Indian Council of Cultural Relations (ICCR)

Preface

Indonesia has always fascinated me. The beauty of the archipelago, the friendly temperament of the people, its religious syncretism and, above all, the immense pride in its glorious past, especially the Hindu-Buddhist heritage, cast a spell on me.

My academic interest in the Indonesian Revolution (1945-1949), especially the extra-ordinary role played by India in mobilising international support, was kindled by the former Indian diplomat P.R.S. Mani. Mani went to Indonesia first as a journalist, and, later as a diplomat. He became friendly with the Indonesian triumvirate – Sukarno, Mohammad Hatta and Sutan Sjahrir – and also became the 'eyes and ears' of Jawaharlal Nehru on matters concerning Indonesia. Long hours that I spent with him, after his retirement, inspired me to do this book.

The younger generation, in Indonesia as well as in India, is unaware of the camaraderie that prevailed among the leaders of the two countries. It is my earnest hope that this publication will provide a necessary corrective and also help promote bilateral relations. The distance between India Point and Pu Breush, a small island located in North West Sumatra, is less than the distance between Chennai and Tirupati. The two countries are so near, yet intellectually remain wide apart.

The book is not an exhaustive study of Indonesian nationalism. My focus is to highlight the inspiration that

Indonesian nationalist leaders derived from India and how New Delhi galvanized international support for the Indonesian Republic.

The 'Foreword' is written by Dr. Vinay Sahasrabuddhe, Member of Parliament and President, Indian Council for Cultural Relations. He is extremely familiar with the subject. My profound gratitude to him.

The illustrations, which have made the book a visual delight, were drawn by Shri Arum Ram Kumar and Smt. Sushmita Vishvanathan. My heartfelt thanks to them.

It is a matter of immense pride to me that the book is being published by Antar Rashtriya Sahayog Paishad. This organization, under the dynamic leadership of Ambassador Virendra Gupta and my good friends, Shri Shyam Parande and Shri Sushil Pandit, is playing a catalytic role in promoting India's cultural relations with outside world, especially the Indian Diasporic communities in the Third World.

Ambassador Anup Mudgal was ever ready to render all assistance.

—V. Suryanarayan

Acknowledgement

This book, to use a term popularized by President Sukarno, is the result of *Gotong Rojong*, mutual co-operation. I have encouraged my students to do research on various aspects of our foreign policy. My intellectual horizon widened while discussing various issues with them. They have consulted several primary sources and I have also made use of them in the preparation of manuscript.

I would like to mention, in particular, Shri Lakshmana Chetty, who read The *Hindu* from 1945 to 1954; consulted the debates of the Central Legislative Council and Constituent Assembly as also the proceedings of the U.N. Security Council and the General Assembly. Nothing gives greater pleasure to a teacher than to see his students rise high in their chosen careers. Dr Lakshmana Chetty became Professor and, subsequently, Director, Centre for Southeast Asian and Pacific Studies, Sri Venkateshwara University, Tirupati. Even after retirement, he is actively associated with the academic programmes of the University.

During the course of my research, I have accumulated several debts. It is a difficult task to name all of them. But, I would like to mention Dr. Balakrishnan N., who retired as Deputy Director from the Nehru Memorial Museum and Library, recently. This Library has the richest collection of material on Modern India. With unfailing courtesy, Balakrishnan assisted me in locating relevant material. He also facilitated my lecture in the Nehru Memorial

Museum and Library last year on "India and the Indonesian Revolution".

Dr. Balakrishnan introduced me to Smt. Jaya Ravindran, Deputy Director, in the National Archives. Jaya made available archival materials dealing with East Indies and Indonesia, My sincere thanks to her.

Among other libraries, which I have consulted, mention should be made of the Library of the Centre for South and Southeast Asian Studies, University of Madras; Library of the Indian Council of World Affairs, New Delhi; Library of the Institute for Defence Studies and Analyses, New Delhi and Library of Jawaharlal Nehru University, New Delhi.

Shri Prem Kumar, Librarian, U.S. Information Services, Chennai, helped me in accessing the internet sources. With an infectious smile, Prem Kumar used to sit by the computer and download valuable material for me. My heartfelt gratitude to Shri Prem Kumar.

I had occasions to interact with two of our former Ambassadors to Indonesia: Ambassador Navrekha Sharma and Ambassador Biren Nanda. I gained immensely from conversations with them. Ambassador Lalith Mansingh, former Foreign Secretary, invited me to participate in an international seminar on India and Indonesia in Bhubaneshwar, where I met many delegates from Indonesia and sought their views on India-Indonesia relations.

Ambassador Fabian K.P., Ambassador Sreenivasan T.P. and Ambassador Ganapathi M. gave me rare insight into the making of our foreign policy. Ambassador Ganapathi read two chapters and made valuable suggestions.

While preparing the manuscript, I received unstinted assistance from several friends, whom I would like to mention: Shri Subramanian K., Shri Sankaran.G, Shri

Raghunathan N. and Smt. Sumathi Raghunathan, Dr. Ashik Bonofer, Smt. Divya Bonofer, Shri Sashi Nair, Dr. Amba Sanjeevi, Shri Sundeep Kumar N., Smt. Srividya Mahesh, Shri Rajgopal Shasti, Dr. Sudhir P., Shri Ramesh, Shri Robin S., Dr. Priya S., Selvi Lavanya R. and Selvi Saranya R. I am thankful to all of them. My brother, Shri Dorai, living in Toronto, not only made incisive comments, but also cautioned against succumbing to the 'Sapru House' habits of cumbersome footnoting and needless quotations.

Smt. Subbalakshmi S. and Smt. Geethanjali S. have always been there to share my joys and sorrows. Without their loving care and affection, this manuscript would never have seen the light of day.

Contents

1
Introduction

On 17 August 1945, Indonesian nationalist leaders, Sukarno and Hatta, proclaimed the independence of Indonesia. The Dutch colonial rule formally ended only on 27 December, 1949. However, it is the earlier date, 17 August, which is considered by the Indonesians as the beginning of their nationhood. The nationalists naturally asserted that independence was a right, and not a matter of grace.

The four years between 1945 and 1949 were turbulent and this period is generally referred to as the Indonesian Revolution. During this time, India was Indonesia's window to the outside world; what is more, New Delhi did play a very significant role in mobilizing international opinion on behalf of the Indonesian people.

A number of scholarly works have been written dealing with the emergence of Indonesian nationalism and the Indonesian struggle for freedom. While the Indonesian nationalist triumvirate – Sukarno, Mohammad Hatta and Sutan Sjahrir – have repeatedly acknowledged India's seminal contributions to the cause of Indonesian independence, Western scholars have generally displayed a marked tendency to minimise India's role. Except for incidental references to Nehru's plan to visit Indonesia (which, though did not take place) and the New Delhi Conference on Indonesia in 1949, even the oft-quoted and widely acclaimed book on Indonesian nationalism, *Nationalism and Revolution in Indonesia*, by Prof. George McT Kahin does not give much credit to India's efforts to mobilize international opinion on behalf of Indonesia. It is all the more saddening because Prof. Kahin was present in Jogjakarta and was an eye-witness to the momentous developments. Late Prof. Benedict Anderson, who considered Indonesia his second home, also errs on the same side. His excellent book, *Java in the Time of Revolution*, suffers from the same shortcoming.

This book is a humble endeavour to set the record straight and to highlight India's role in the Indonesian struggle for independence. I hope it will help to generate interest among young generations, both in India and in Indonesia, and also help to foster better India-Indonesia relations. In the *Ramayana*, there is the story of the squirrel, which also contributes in its small way to the construction of the *Ram Sethu*. The squirrel finally got the blessings of Lord Rama. I hope my efforts will also receive recognition from the scholarly community committed to the promotion of India-Indonesia relations.

I went to Indonesia in October 2010 to participate in an international conference on "The Cultural and Historical Links between India and Southeast Asia". The conference was arranged in two venues – University of Indonesia in Jakarta and Gajamada University in Jogjakarta. The audience consisted mainly of faculty and students. I was deeply distressed to note that the younger generation in Indonesia was not conversant with India-Indonesia relations, especially during the 1940's and 1950's. Indian specialists in Indonesian studies should make sincere efforts to remedy the situation.

Pioneers in Building Bridges of Understanding

My interest in India's role in Indonesian revolution was kindled by former Indian diplomat P. R. S. Mani. I met Mani for the first time in India International Centre, New Delhi in a seminar on Indian Communities in Southeast Asia organized by Ambassador I. J. Bahadur Singh. Though I had heard of Mani's professional career, I was not aware of his deep involvement in the Indonesian Revolution. I invited him to my Centre in the University of Madras to speak to the faculty and students on India and the Indonesian Revolution. I also persuaded Mani to give me the manuscript of his lectures, which the University of Madras later published as a Monograph in 1986 entitled *The Story of Indonesian Revolution*. A few years later, Mani acknowledged that, on the basis of the Monograph, a book was published in *Bahasa* Indonesia entitled *Jelak Revolusi* 1945, *sebuah kesaksian sejarah*.

The well-known Indonesian diplomat, Roeslan Abdulgani, reviewed the book in *Tempo*. The review was translated into English and published in *Indonesia Quarterly*. Few lines from the review are worth quoting:

> The influence of the three revolutionary leaders made a deep impression on Mani's personality, namely, Sukarno with his charisma, the quiet and polite Hatta with his intellectual; aptitude; Sjahrir, with his analytical and keen thoughts. Sukarno cautiously fanned the revolutionary spirit; Hatta used his position with the Japanese Government to maintain it in disguise. And Sjahrir organized and directed the revolutionary spirit along with the faithful groups of students in support.

A few words would be of relevance about Mani's involvement with Southeast Asia in general and Indonesia in particular. As a student in Madras Christian College, P. R. Subramanyam got deeply interested in the Indian national movement. After graduation, he became a radio journalist in the All India Radio in 1940; in 1942, he was transferred to the Head Quarters in New Delhi. He shortened his name to P. R. S. Mani, by which name he was known in later life. Mani was an army observer in Manipur, when it came under Japanese attack. He was sent to East Indies to report on the Japanese surrender. Mani's heart was with the Indonesian nationalists and he soon realized that he could not report according to the dictates of his conscience. To quote Mani: "A thousand regrets I am not a free correspondent to report what I observe". He, therefore, resigned from the army and returned to India. Mani then contacted the legendary journalist, Sadanand, who appointed him as the correspondent of the *Free Press Journal.*

Mani accompanied Jawaharlal Nehru during his visit to Malaya and Singapore in March 1946. They developed mutual respect and it can rightly be said that Mani became the eyes and ears of Jawaharlal Nehru on matters concerning the Indonesian Republic. After Indian independence, Nehru persuaded Mani to join the Indian Foreign Service and posted him as the press relations officer in the Indian Embassy in Jogjakarta. Mani's dispatches, which are available in the National Archives, are a mine of information on the Indonesian Revolution. He also worked in the Secretariat of the Asian Relations Conference, 1947 and Conference on Indonesia, 1949.

On 17 August,, 1946, the Indonesian Republic celebrated its first anniversary of the proclamation of Indonesian independence. Navrekha Sharma, who was

Indian Ambassador in Indonesia from 2006 to 2008, has written in her book (co-author Prof. Baladas Ghoshal), *IndiaÕs Relations withIndonesia*, that the Indian national flag was hoisted along with Indonesia's flag, *Marah Putih* (Red and White flag of the Indonesian Republic). Obviously, the statement is not completely right. The national tri-color flag of India was adopted in the Constituent Assembly on 22 July 1947 and was first hoisted on Indian Independence Day, 15 August 1947. Presumably the tri-color flag of the Indian National Congress was hoisted along with the flag of the Indonesian Republic.

President Sukarno complimented Mani by name in his *Merdeka* (independence) day speech and thanked him for his support to the Indonesian cause. Sukarno added, "That is why when P. R. S. Mani asked Dr. Sutan Sjahrir whether Indonesia would help India with rice, we agreed without any hesitation whatsoever". Nehru also praised P. R. S. Mani for his sincere efforts to promote India-Indonesia relations. In a letter to Mani, Nehru wrote, "My dear Mani, you are doing good work in Indonesia and I hope you will continue it. I wish we could send someone else to Java, but at present I see no way to do it". In later years, Mani served in Manila, Shanghai, Hong Kong, Goa, West Germany, Nepal, Sri Lanka, Mauritius and Sweden, from where he retired as Ambassador. I want to place on record my sincere gratitude to P. R. S. Mani for kindling my interest in the Indonesian Revolution. As a token of my love, respect and affection, I dedicate this book to his memory.

Closely associated with P.R.S. Mani was his contemporary in Madras Christian College T.G. Narayanan. Narayanan was the *Hindu* correspondent in Southeast Asia and covered the developments in Indonesia in great detail. He was very friendly with Sukarno, Hatta and Sjahrir and persuaded them to write for the *Hindu*. Later, he joined the United Nations and wrote the backgrounder on Indonesia for the benefit of U.N. officials who were at that time mediating between the Indonesian nationalists and the Dutch Government. At the time of his demise, Narayanan was personal assistant to U.N. Secretary General Dag Hammarskjold.

The third great Indian who supported the Indonesian national movement was Bijoyananda Patnaik, popularly known as Biju Patnaik. During his student days, he had come under the spell of Jawaharlal Nehru, participated in the Quit India movement and was imprisoned by the British for his anti-British activities. Later, he was trained as a pilot and started the Kalinga Airlines. While working in the National Archives, I was very happy to find in the catalogue a file entitled Biju Patnaik. I was very eager to see the contents. I made a formal request for the file, but was greatly disappointed the next day when the slip was returned with the comment N. T. not transferred.

Patnaik used to regularly fly to the Republican territory carrying much needed medicines. He became extremely friendly with the nationalist triumvirate. He brought Sjahrir to the Asian Relations Conference in his Dakota. When Meghawati Sukarnoputri visited India as the President of Indonesia, she recalled that when her birth was conveyed to her father, Patnaik was keeping company with Sukarno. The name Meghawati – daughter of the clouds - was suggested by Patnaik. When the Dutch were planning a military attack on Jogjakarta, Sukarno was very keen that Mohammad Hatta should come out of Indonesia. Hatta travelled with Patnaik as his co-pilot and was named Abdullah. The plane flew to New Delhi via Kuala Lumpur and Rangoon. After arriving in New Delhi, Hatta established contacts with Nehru.

Patnaik was a dare devil and never sought permission

of the Government of India or the Republican Government before undertaking his flying missions. The Republican leaders were very keen to overcome the Dutch blockade. Biju Patnaik prepared a blueprint to go to Jogjakarta from India without touching the Dutch colonial possessions. The route was – Calcutta – Rangoon – Mergui - Kutaraja – Jogjakarta. Patnaik approached the Government of India for financial support. Unfortunately, due to bureaucratic red tape, the plan could not be implemented. When it was certain that the Dutch forces would capture Jogjakarta in 1948, the Indonesian nationalist leaders were very keen to establish a Government in exile in New Delhi. Sukarno and Hatta were to have come to India, while Sjahrir was to have gone to Sumatra. Unfortunately, the plane which was kept ready by Patnaik to go to Indonesia to fly Sukarno and Hatta to India could not reach Republican territory because of Dutch blockade. A grateful Indonesian nation conferred the title of *Bhumiputra* (son of the soil) and offered Patnaik a "royal salute" in July 1980.

Mention should also be made of the contributions made by Mohammad Yunus, who was India's first Consul in Jogjakarta. Yunus was the disciple of Khan Abdul Ghaffar Khan, "Frontier Gandhi" as he was known, and was a great friend of the Nehru family. Yunus shared with Sukarno qualities of intense nationalism, secularism, sense of humour and a zest for life. President Sukarno and Mohammad Yunus became close friends. In his book, *Persons, Passions and Politics*, Mohammad Yunus mentions that he was known in Indonesia as Bung *Yunus dari India* (Brother Yunus from India). So great was Sukarno's faith in Mohammad Yunus that he used to ask Yunus to accompany him to cabinet meetings. The Indian Consulate in Jogjakarta was the main window through which the Indonesian leaders established contacts with the outside world. Yunus made available telegraphic facilities for the use of the Republican leaders. This was intended to prevent the Dutch from disrupting important messages. The Indonesian admiration for Mohammad Yunus was so great that President Sukarno gave a letter of appreciation for his great work in promoting India-Indonesia relations.

In 1995, the Government of Indonesia honoured four Indians with the award of *Bintang Jasa Uthama* – The First Class Star of Service. The four Indians were: 1) Jawaharlal Nehru; 2) P R S Mani; 3) Biju Patnaik and 4) Mohammad Yunus.

Heather Goodall, Australian scholar, who has specialized in Indonesia, has written an article entitled "Writing Conflicted Loyalties: An Indian Journalist's Perspectives on the Dilemmas of Indian Troops in Indonesia, 1945". She also organized an exhibition on "P. R. S. Mani: An Indian Journalist in Indonesia" in Nehru Memorial Museum and Library. Unfortunately she has mentioned that Mohammad Yunus was awarded the Nobel Prize. It is a clear case of mistaken identity.

Indonesia Acknowledges India's Role

The nationalist movement in Indonesia was, essentially, an Indonesian response to imperialist domination. It developed its own nuances and methods of struggle depending on the ideological orientation of the leadership, the policies and programmes of the colonial government and the compulsion of events. At the same time, as the largest imperialist possession in Asia, which was waging a heroic struggle in a non-violent manner against British domination, the Indian nationalist movement inspired the nationalist leaders of Asian countries. As Sukarno, father of the Indonesian nation, put it:

Nehru and Sukarno

> India and Gandhi frequently inspired me and our struggle for freedom and, in those lonely years, when I had been exiled from my own people or confined to death prison cell, only because I sought freedom of my people, it was my strong belief in God and the inspiring spirit of India that raised my hopes and my own faith in our cause.

Another memorable quotation of Sukarno would not be out of place. After the successful ten-day visit of Jawaharlal Nehru to Indonesia in June 1950, when Sukarno accompanied Nehru throughout, Nehru sent a message to the people of Indonesia expressing his gratitude to them. Sukarno followed it with his own message. To quote Sukarno:

> For the past ten days I had the privilege of continuous personal contact with and the continuous company of Panditji. This has tended to strengthen our personal relations of long standing and my respect for him has grown. As a friend, as an intellectual, and as a man, I have found in him a true friend of Indonesia and you are fortunate indeed to have him as your leader.

In a letter dated 20 April, 1948, addressed to "My dearest Bhai" (Jawaharlal Nehru), Mohammad Yunus, Indian Consul in Jogjakarta, referred to his conversation with Sukarno, wherein the President, to quote Yunus' words, said, "Delhi is the centre of our hopes and the nerve centre of the east".

This is made clear in Mohammad Hattta's views on the significance of India in the Indonesian struggle for independence. In a letter dated 1 December, 1945, to Jawaharlal Nehru, Hatta, after explaining the machinations of the Dutch Government, to perpetuate colonial rule, concluded:

> To a certain extent, our chance depends on the developments in India. If India will soon be free, Indonesia will soon follow because there is no more interest for the British to support the Dutch claim. Without British support, the Dutch have no power enough to impose their rule on a hostile population. So it is a matter of great importance if India and Indonesia could establish a close relationship in our common struggle against capitalism and imperialism.

Notable are the views of Sutan Sjahrir expressed soon after Jawaharlal Nehru's demise. From the prison cell, Sjahrir wrote:

> Panditji, together with the Mahatma, will live on as spiritual and moral guides in the great Asian and human endeavour. We Indonesians, in particular, shall always gratefully remember the role that Panditji played in our struggle for independence.... And above all, in the minds and hearts of Indonesian people, also for generations to come, Pandit Jawaharlal Nehru will continue to be cherished and loved as a staunch and faithful ally, who stood by us, and who did everything possible to aid and assist us during the most crucial and decisive periods of the Indonesian struggle for Independence.

Similar Problems, Identical Approach

An important factor that brought India and Indonesia closer together must be highlighted. The two countries faced similar problems and they pursued more or less the same policies to tackle these problems. India and Indonesia were two countries, where nationalist leaders, as a matter of deliberate choice, rejected majority religion as the basis of nationhood and resolved to make their countries secular states. However, there is one major difference. The word secular does not find a mention in the *Pancasila* Constitution. It highlights that every Indonesian has the right to believe "in his own particular God".

India and Indonesia did not subscribe to the policy

of cultural homogenization. They pursued policies which respected both diversities and linkages. In India, the motto is "unity in diversity"; in Indonesia It is *Bhinneka Tungal Ika*, though divided we are one.

The two countries were also determined to face squarely the problems posed by religious extremists. In Indonesia, the extreme section of the Moslem community rallied behind Darul Islam and championed the cause of a state strictly based on Islamic principles. Some of them proclaimed the formation of an independent state, the Republic of South Moluccas. The Darul Islam had some following in South Moluccas, West Java and Sulawesi. The secular nationalists faced the challenge ideologically and militarily. (Indonesia did not uphold laws based on Shariah). The same trends can be discerned in India. It is well known that both Nehru and Gandhiji stood like rocks against religious extremism. In the dark days following the partition of India, it was the determination of these two leaders that saved the minority communities. However, one difference should be highlighted. It would have been better if India had also codified the Mohammadan Law as it did in the case of Hindus; but the Indian nationalist leadership bent backwards and decided to wait till such time the demand came from the Muslim community itself.

In Indonesia, as well as in India, the communist parties resorted to armed struggles for capturing power. Musso, Communist leader, returned from Soviet Union and began to propagate the thesis that the only solution to the manifold problems facing the infant Republic was the establishment of a communist state through forcible capture of power. In an interview with Prof. George McT Kahin, Sukarno said that Musso and Amir, made political capital from the fact those negotiations with the Dutch "had produced nothing".

Sukarno added that if the nationalists had arrived at a political settlement and the Dutch had lifted the economic blockade the "basis of communist appeal" would have disappeared.

How unrealistic the communist leadership was can be understood from the fact that the Party even branded the highly respected Sultan of Jogjakarta, Hemengku Buwono, as the running dog of imperialists. The Dutch offered their assistance to the Republican leaders to tackle the communist revolt, which started from Madium. The Republican leaders rejected the offer. Attempts made by the *Partai Kommunis Indonesia* (P.K.I.) to establish *Tanah Merah* (Red Earth) miserably failed. It was only after the elimination of the Communist Party, the United States recognized the nationalist credentials of the Republican leaders.

Students of Indonesian foreign policy can discern the origins of non-alignment in Indonesian foreign policy to this period. The United States, after the Second World War, extended its support to Holland to re-impose colonial rule in East Indies. Moscow also did not have a high opinion of the Indonesian nationalists. Naturally, instead of aligning itself with the two power blocs, Indonesia, in the words of Vice-President Mohammad Hatta, in September 1948, began to advocate an "active and independent" foreign policy. Mohammad Hatta has elucidated why Indonesia chose not to join any power blocs. To quote Hatta:

> The foreign policy of the Republic of Indonesia is not one of neutrality, because it is not constructed in reference to belligerent states but for the purpose of strengthening and upholding peace. Indonesia plays no favourites between the two opposed power blocs

> and follows its own path through the various international problems. It terms this policy "independent" and further characterizes it by describing it as independent and 'active'.

The independent and active approach to foreign policy naturally brought India and Indonesia closer.

Transfer of Power: Compromise Formula

The transfer of power from Holland to Indonesia which took place in 1949 was based on a compromise formula. Power was transferred to United States of Indonesia, a federal union in which the Republic was only one component. The Republican leaders, and the armed forces, considered it as capitulation. They viewed it as a colonial device to balkanize Indonesia. In the detailed discussions that I had with P.R.S. Mani on the subject, I learnt that Jawaharlal Nehru advised Mohammad Hatta, the chief negotiator for the Republic, to accept the compromise formula, otherwise the colonial rule might continue in the archipelago. The Indian experience was cited; the nationalist leaders had to accept partition of the sub-continent as a price to be paid for independence. Nehru also added that once the transfer of power took place, the puppet federal units would burst like a soap bubble. This prophecy turned out to be true. The United States of Indonesia, which was established on 27 December, 1949, was dissolved and a unitary state of Indonesia came into existence on 17 August 1950.

❑

2

India And Indonesia–Cultural Interaction

India does not evoke memories of an imperialist past in Southeast Asian minds. Except the Chola naval expedition in the early 11th century, which did not have any lasting impact, the interaction had been benign which resulted in the cultural efflorescence of the region. Describing the spread of Indian cultural influences, Jawaharlal Nehru has written in *Discovery of India*: “Just as Hellenism spread from Greece to the countries of the Mediterranean and in Western Asia, India’s cultural influences spread to many countries and left a powerful impress upon them”. Take Indonesia as an illustration. Indianised kingdoms like Sri Vijaya, Mataram, Sailendra, Singosari and Majapahit; popularity of Agastya cult in Java; familiar Indian words in Bahasa Indonesia; architectural monuments like Borobudur and Lara Djonggrang; literary masterpieces like Amaramala, Arjuna Vijaya and Bharata Yuddha; the *Wajang Kulit* based on the Ramayana and Mahabharata themes; the living Indian traditions in the Island of Bali – all these are testimony to the courage and zeal of Indian princes, poets, priests, merchants and artisans and the assimilable qualities of the people of Indonesia.

Agastya

Let me illustrate this point. In addition to variety of Ramayana tellings in different parts of the archipelago, the great Indian epic has influenced literature, performing arts, and moral and political philosophy. As Malini Saran and Vinod Khanna have highlighted in their book, The *Ramayana in Indonesia*:

> These range from the millennium-old sculptural masterpieces in the temples of Lara Djonggrang (Prambanan) to the spectacular enactment today in an open air amphitheatre with the same temples illuminated in the background; from poetic rendition of the late nineteenth century old Javanese Ramayana *Kakawain* to the allegorical use of the Ramayana in the overthrow of President Suharto.

The Indonesian nationalist leaders have frequently made appreciative references to fruitful cultural interaction their country had with India. As President Sukarno wrote in a special article in *The Hindu* dated 4 January, 1945:

> In the veins of every one of my people flows the blood of Indian ancestors and the culture that we possess is seeped through and through with Indian influences. Two thousand years ago, people from your country came to Yavadvipa and Suvarnadvipa in the spirit of brotherly love. They gave the initiative to found powerful Kingdoms such as those of Sri Vijaya, Mataram and Majapahit. We learnt then to worship the very Gods that you worship still and we fashioned a culture that even today is largely identical with your own. Later, we turned to Islam, but that religion too was brought to us by people coming from both sides of the Indus.

I want to give another illustration of Sukarno's acknowledgement of cultural indebtedness to India. In a letter, dated 19 August 1946, to Jawaharlal Nehru, following the first anniversary of the proclamation of the Indonesian Republic, Sukarno wrote:

> Your country and your people are linked to us by ties of blood and culture which date back to the very beginning of history. The word "India" must necessarily always be part of our life for it forms the first two syllables of the name we have chosen…for our land and our race… it is the "Indo" in Indonesia. This Jogjakarta from which I write is – like Java, Sumatra and most other place names – an Indian word; my very name is eloquent testimony to the great extent to which we have fallen heir to the rich culture of your ancient land.

The spread of Indian cultural influences, leading to the cultural enrichment of Southeast Asian countries, constitutes a glorious chapter in Indian and Southeast Asian history. The famous lines of Rabindranath Tagore, who visited Indonesia in 1927, come to my mind:

> In the dim, distant unrecorded age
> we had met, thou and I
> when my speech tangled in thine
> and my life in thy life…
>
> From the heavens spoke to me two mighty voices
> the one that sung of Rama's glory of sorrow

> and the other of Arjuna's triumphant arms
> urging me to bear along with the waves
> this epic lines in the eastern islands;
> and the heart of my hand murmured to me its hope
> that it might build its nest of love
> in a far away land of its dream.

Jawaharlal Nehru was enthralled during his visit to the island of Bali in June 1950, which left behind "indelible impressions". I am tempted to quote Nehru's words, extracted from a letter written to the Chief Ministers, on 2 July 1950:

> The island of Bali is famous for many things and it lived up to its reputation. There is an enchantment about it, which affected me all the more, because of its living culture, derived much from India from the distant past. I have never come across a more artistic people than the people of Bali. Artistry was at the tip of their fingers and in the toes of their feet. Every man, woman and child seems to be born with this sense of beauty and grace.

Even when strains developed in India-Indonesia relations in later years, Sukarno never disowned his country's cultural indebtedness to India. The eminent danseuse Dr. Padma Subramaniam is fond of narrating an interesting incident. When Z. A. Bhutto tried to build close relations with Indonesia on the basis of Islamic solidarity, Sukarno told Bhutto: "Yes, I am a Muslim by faith, but I am a Hindu by cultural inheritance".

Bali Yatra

The benign contacts between India and Southeast Asia are closely intertwined with the folklore and festivals in different parts of India. For example, in the coastal state of Odisha, every year on the *Karthik Poornima* day (full moon day in the month of *Karthik*) people float boats made out of paper, banana tree barks or corks, with an oil lamp inside it, and let them float in tanks and rivers after sun set. The festival commemorates the voyage undertaken by their ancestors to Indonesian archipelago, making use of favourable winds. The festival received a boost when Biju Patnaik was the Chief Minister of Odisha. It acts as a reminder of their rich maritime heritage, when the more adventurous among them set sail to distant Bali. In 1992-93, the Government of Odisha re-enacted the ancient voyage from Kalinga to Bali, with the INS Samudra sailing from Paradeep to Bali.

Cultural Syncretism

How does one explain the harmonious co-existence of Islamic faith with Hindu and animist traditions in Indonesia? The answer lies in cultural syncretism, which is a unique characteristic of Indonesian way of life through the ages. The Indonesian mind believes in synthesis and is accustomed to the intermingling of diverse and apparently contradictory elements. The average Indonesian finds no dichotomy in his obligations as a Moslem and his continued acceptance of earlier Hindu and animist practices. As Prof. Clifford Geertz has pointed out, in his book, *Religion of Java*:

> The propitiation of spirits, the observance of customary rituals surrounding the main stages of life, the resort to magical practices in curing

> illness may all be accepted by the same person, who is ready to observe the Moslem law of marriage, to accept the Muslim ritual of circumcision, or to follow the daily pattern of prayer, the weekly community worship, and the annual month of fasting.

The first great religion to arrive in Indonesia was Hinduism and it was soon followed by the Mahayana form of Buddhism. Before Hinduism arrived, the people of the islands were animists. The new religions did not compete for people's support; they blended with native animism and assumed new shapes. Siva merged with the Buddha and the cult of Siva-Buddha came into existence. In most parts of Indonesia the Banyan tree is still considered sacred and never cut down. Similarly, at the time of harvest, each stalk of paddy has to be cut in a different fashion and as quietly as possible, to avoid disturbing *Devi Sri*, the guardian spirit of fertility. Belief in magic is quite common and the *Kris*, short ceremonial dagger, is endowed with magical powers and is worshipped every day.

Islam came to Indonesia in the 15th century and it spread throughout the archipelago in the course of the next three hundred years. It was brought by the merchants of Gujarat, who were followers of the Sufi variant of Islam and had already undergone changes in the direction of mysticism, which facilitated its adoption and adaptation in the Indonesian setting.

Recent researches have proved that in the transmission of Islam to Indonesia and Malaysia, Muslims from other parts of India have also played significant roles. As Prof. Arun Das Gupta, who was Professor for Indian Studies in the University of Indonesia, Jakarta during 1979-

81, has pointed out that there were multiple sources of islamisation. In addition to the Gujarati Muslims, Muslims from Tamil Nadu and Kerala, Bengal and even Arabia have played significant roles. There was a close link between trade and Islamisation; wherever the Muslim traders went they carried the Islamic faith with them. There was big concentration of Muslim trading settlements in Malacca, Acheh and Makassar.

Distinguished sociologist Clifford Geertz explains the religion of Java as follows:

> Indonesian Islam, cut off from the centres of orthodoxy in Mecca and Cairo, vegetated another meandering tropical growth on an already overcrowded religious landscape. Buddhist mystic practices got Arabic names, the Hindu Rajas suffered a change of title to become Muslim Sultans; and the common people called some of their spirits Jinns; but little else changed.

One of the first books that I read on Indonesia, as a research scholar in New Delhi, was a book entitled *Story of Indonesia* by Louis Fischer. Writing about the impact of Islam on Indonesia, he mentions that "Rama went to Mecca and came back as Mohammad". J. D. Legge, biographer of Sukarno, mentions that Sukarno told an American journalist that he was "simultaneously a Christian, a Muslim and a Hindu".

The well-known Islamic scholar, Asghar Ali Engineer, who visited Indonesia several times, has highlighted an important dimension of Indonesian traditions. In his book, *Living Faith*, Engineer writes about his visit to Gadjah

Mada University to participate in a seminar. Engineer was received by two Indonesian Moslem girls in the Jogjakarta airport, whose names were Sita and Lakshmi. A surprised Engineer was told by his hosts that Sita and Lakshmi were common names among Indonesian Moslems. They also told Engineer that when a Moslem woman becomes pregnant she is given a coconut with the images of a man and a woman engraved on it, signifying that if a girl is born she is like Sita and if a boy is born he be like Rama. Engineer also refers to a conversation he had with Islamic scholar, Abdul Rahman Wahid, who later became the President of Indonesia. Wahid told Engineer, "Do you know the name of the greatest preacher of Islam in Indonesia? His name is Maulana Vishnu".

Concept of Greater India – Need for Re-Assessment

It is high time that Indian scholars started re-evaluating concepts like Greater India, Hindu colonies and Hinduisation. These concepts evolved during the Indian national movement with the formation of Greater India Society in Calcutta. It definitely gave us a sense of pride in our history. At the same time, it must be pointed out that its leading protagonists, more often not, adopted a patronising tone and denied Southeast Asian cultures autonomy of their own. To cite one illustration, Prof. R. C. Majumdar has written:

> On the whole it is difficult to avoid the conclusion that Indian cultural influence deeply penetrated the soul of diverse races in Asia over widely extended regions and enabled them in many cases to emerge out of primitive barbarism.

Ambassador Badr-ud-Din Tyabji, who was Indian

Ambassador in Indonesia during the late 1950s, expands on the patronizing tone of the Indian visitors to Indonesia. To quote from his book, *Memoirs of an Egotist*:

> Unfortunately many Indians...would even go to the extent of teaching the Indonesians how to pronounce their own names and institutions in the correct classical Sanskrit manner. The Indonesians reacted badly to this crude form of cultural chauvinism.

People of Southeast Asia had developed a high degree of civilization even before India established cultural contacts with Southeast Asia. Therefore, students of history feel deeply hurt when writers like R C. Majumdar turn a "Nelsons eye" to indigenous cultural traits. It should be pointed out that in the early phase of Southeast Asian history geo-political boundaries were fluid, porous and inter-penetrating. During the nationalist phase, the theory of one-directional cultural penetration took place. As Prof. Arun Das Gupta has pointed out, instead of looking at Southeast Asia as an extension of India, we must start looking at the region as a "Sangam" where several cultural influences mingled and created something unique. Prof. Arun Das Gupta sums it up in the following words. The concept of Greater India, in its older form,

> is not very useful. This does not mean we have to reject the unquestionable evidence of tremendous Indian influence in Southeast Asia. I suggest that instead of looking at Southeast Asian culture as an extension of Indian culture, we should treat the Southeast Asian region as a confluence area.

This balanced historical approach alone will give a fillip to India-Southeast Asia relations. I am left with mixed feelings. When I think of the enormous efforts that have gone to the study of the cultural evolution of Southeast Asian societies, I am left with mixed feelings. Is the glass half empty or half full? The Indian scholars, committed to Southeast Asian Studies, should ponder over what Prof. Van Leur wrote about Dutch historiography, “The writing of real history has yet to begin”.

Study in Contrast

Located to the east of India and to the South of China, Southeast Asian countries, naturally, were subjected to cultural influences from the two great Asian countries. A comparative study highlights the contrasting ways in which cultural influences spread. The Indian influences are all pervasive; as Jawaharlal Nehru said, in the course of his visit to Cambodia, in 1954 “every blade of grass breathes Indian culture”. And these influences spread, as mentioned earlier, through peaceful means. In contrast, the spread of Chinese cultural influences in the northern part of Vietnam was due to political subjugation and consequent sinicisation.

The struggle against Chinese domination was a recurring theme in Vietnamese history. The two great national heroes of Vietnam are the Trung sisters, who rallied the people and fought against Chinese domination. The Trung sisters, Trung Trac and Trung Nhi, were daughters of a powerful Vietnamese landlord, who lived in the first century A D. Vietnam was under the rule of the Han dynasty. Vietnamese women enjoyed more freedom than their Chinese counterparts. China was governed by Confucian values, where women were subordinate to men.

Feeling oppressed by the Chinese rule, the Vietnamese were exhorted to revolt and the Trung sisters organized a rebellion and formed an army of 80,000 men and women. They won back the territory conquered by the Chinese. In 42 A. D., Chinese forces were sent to re-conquer the lost territory. The Vietnamese fought hard and were to be defeated. According to popular belief, the Trung sisters decided to take their lives in the traditional manner by jumping into the river and drowning. They became symbols of Vietnamese resistance. Temples were later built in their honour and the people of Vietnam celebrate their memory every year with a national holiday.

Visible Symbols

The influence of Ramayana in Southeast Asia has already been referred to. It is not only the epic of India; it is also the national epic of Indonesia. Ramayana had been a perennial source of inspiration in the past and continues to exercise its charm and fascination even today. The simple story of Rama and Sita had been told and retold a million times in different parts of the archipelago. No doubt, in the process of its diffusion and transplantation, the Ramayana has undergone variations and adaptations. The immense vitality of the Ramayana tradition in contemporary Indonesia is a proof, if a proof is necessary, to the aptness of Brahma's assurance to Valmiki. "And O' great sage, as long as the mountains stand, and the rivers flow, so long will the story of Rama's heroic deeds be told and cherished on earth". As the former Indian diplomat, K. M. Kannampilly, has written:

> For over fourteen centuries now, the Ramayana has continued to be a living force among the people of Southeast Asia, influencing their hearts

> and thoughts, inspiring their artistic creations and forming the mainspring of their cultural life. To them the hero and heroine of Ramayana have always been models of chivalry, nobility and faithfulness, characters of great spiritual beauty.

Even in the world of scholarship relating to the Ramayana tradition, Indonesia has played a pioneering role. The Ministry of Information and Culture organized the first international Ramayana festival in Jakarta in August-September 1971. Scholars and artists from India, Indonesia, Sri Lanka, Nepal, Malaysia, Singapore, Philippines, Vietnam, Laos and Cambodia, participated in this unique seminar whose objective was "to promote deeper cultural understanding amongst nations". Four years later, in 1975, New Delhi picked up the threads and on the occasion of the 400th anniversary of *Ramcharitamanas* of Tulsidas, organized an international seminar on "Ramayana Tradition in Asia". The Sahitya Academy again convened another international seminar on "Asian Variations of Ramayana" in January 1981. These seminars and published proceedings are significant milestones in our understanding of the many- splendoured Ramayana tradition.

What is great about Indonesia is the fact that the leadership do not shy away from publicizing their glorious heritage. President Sukarno was named after the Mahabharata hero Karna. Since Karna was in the bad company of the Kauravas, Sukarno's father added a Su to it which means good. The Government of Indonesia has issued innumerable stamps featuring Ramayana and Mahabharata heroes. The Indonesian Airlines is known as Garuda (vehicle of Vishnu) Airlines. Ramayana was translated into *Kawi* language even before Kamba Ramayana was published in 1200 AD. The Central Bank of Indonesia is named after the Hindu God of wealth Kubera. Sage Agastya's statues are found in different parts of Java. Hanuman is the official mascot of Indonesian military intelligence. In the 1977 Asian Games, held in Jakarta, the official mascot was Hanuman.

When you travel down from Sukarno-Hatta international airport to the *Merdeka* Square, you come across several beautiful sculpted figures from Hindu mythology, Bhima, Garuda and Hanuman. But the most beautiful among them, is the depiction of *Arjuna Vijaya* in which God Krishna and Arjuna are in a chariot. This beautiful piece of sculpture was constructed during the Suharto regime. Equally magnificent is the statue of Goddess Saraswathi which adorns the front portion of the Indonesian Embassy in Washington DC. As a token of my admiration to the Indonesian genius, sketches of *Arjuna Vijaya* and *Saraswati.* are given on both sides of the book's cover. They are not reproductions; the artist has allowed his imagination to make additions and deletions to convey the essence.

The question naturally arises: Why do we in India shy away from giving due recognition to our great heroes of the past? Another intriguing aspect of New Delhi's policy towards our Southeast Asian neighbours should be highlighted. In the early years of independence, when the diplomatic enclave was being planned, Nehru told his Secretary T.V. Pai that we should name the diplomatic enclave and its main roads after important events and names in our great history. So the diplomatic enclave was named *Chanakyapuri*. Roads were named Dharma *Marg, Satya Marg, Vinay Marg* and *Shanti* Path. So close was Indonesia to India, the land, very near to *Teen Murti House*, was allotted to Indonesia for the construction of their Embassy. In the course of a conversation, P. R. S. Mani told me in jest that Nehru told Dr. Soedarsono, Indonesian Representative in India, that if he spoke loudly Soedarsono should be able to hear him from his Chancery.

In subsequent years, important roads in the capital were named after Nelson Mandela, Joseph Tito and Archbishop Makarios. Strangely, no road has been named after the great nationalist leaders from Southeast Asia. Sukarno, Hatta, Sjahrir, General Aung San, U Nu, Ho Chih Minh, Sihanouk and Tunku Abdul Rahman - none of them have been given recognition in our capital. When will our leaders set the record straight?

❑

3
Imperialist Phase

The fruitful and benign interaction, referred to in the earlier chapter, underwent a fundamental transformation during the period of European domination over Asia. Basing themselves in India, the British extended their control to Burma, the Straits Settlements and the Malay States. The British were keen to extend their sway to the East Indies also, but in the Anglo-Dutch rivalry for the control of the archipelago, the Dutch emerged victorious. For a short spell during the Napoleonic wars, the East Indies came under the control of the East India Company, but the territory was ceded back to the Dutch under the Paris Peace Settlement.

Lord Curzon, Viceroy of India (1899-1905), referred to India "as the determining influence of every considerable movement in the British power to the east and south of the Mediterranean". In an address to the Guild Hall, London, Curzon explained India's contribution to the expansion of the British Empire. Whether for the protection of the British possessions in Natal, or defending the White man in Peking or fighting the mad Mullah in Somaliland, the British found that the Indian armed forces did the job with great loyalty. The Indian soldiers were effectively used for the defense of British possessions in Asia and Africa. In the same way, Indian labor was fully exploited to develop the plantations and roads and railways in different parts of the Empire.

Indian Community in Indonesia

A few Indian migrants went to Sumatra in the early 20th century to provide the much-needed labour for the development of rubber plantations. The Indian community in Indonesia today number roughly about 50,000 and they live in perfect harmony with the local people. They do not create misgivings and suspicions among the indigenous community like the numerically larger, economically powerful and culturally exclusive Chinese.

The era of imperialism also led to the development of new forms of economic linkages between British India and Dutch East Indies. East Indies became an important source for the supply of certain essential items like sugar, tea, petroleum and tin. India, in turn, exported large quantities of gunny bags, textiles and coal.

Bengal Renaissance

The domination by different colonial masters created a wide wall of separation and prevented co-operation among the peoples of Asia. Even so, in the 19th century, a few Indian intellectuals were sensitive to the common colonial experience and the necessity to instill a pan-Asian consciousness among the peoples of Asia. Kesab Chandra Sen, the great leader from Bengal, tried to impress upon his followers that India must be viewed as an integral part of the Asian world. These pan-Asian sentiments were carried forward by Swami Vivekananda who visited Japan and other Asian countries in 1893. Vivekananda highlighted the common points of Asian cultural heritage and tried to revive the age-old contacts between India and the neighbouring countries of Asia.

Bengal was the first to respond to the British imperialist challenge. There was an intellectual ferment and a new group of writers, artists, social reformers and nationalists emerged and spoke of the necessity for India to re-discover itself. Known as Bengal Renaissance, it was more influential than the *Boedi Utomo* in Indonesia and May 4th Movement in China. Rabindranath Tagore, who established the Visva Bharati in 1921, wanted to combine the best of Western and Indian systems and provide education through English medium. Tagore gave highest priority to education. No wonder, Gandhiji called him *Gurudeva*, the great teacher.

Tagore's Visit to Indonesia, 1927

Tagore was a widely travelled poet; he went on foreign tours as many as twelve times. He was inspired by the tremendous Indian influences in Southeast Asia and wanted to have a direct experience of it. The visit to Indonesia was to "re-discover" Indian cultural links and whether an "Asian cultural identity" could be promoted. Tagore landed in Batavia on 21 August and toured the archipelago; on 30 September he returned to India via Siam, Tagore was accompanied by three well-known Bengali intellectuals – Dr. Suniti Kumar Chatterjee, the well known linguist; Surendranath Kar, artist and architect and Dhirendra Krishna Deva Burman, painter and musician. To avoid embarrassment to the Dutch, Tagore assured the Government that he would keep away from politics.

Krishna Kripalani, the biographer of Tagore, has written that Tagore was "moved deeply, as much because of the natural beauty of the country and the charm of the people and on account of the joy of recognizing an ancient kinship in culture". Tagore was delighted to discover that the Brahma, Vishnu and Siva temples in Prambanan "contained in their terrace walls sculptured reliefs of Ramayana scenes, the likes of which were not to be found in any Indian temples".

Tagore, as Prof. Sugata Bose has pointed out, was undoubtedly

> a powerful critic of worshipping the nation as God and was horrified by the crimes committed by modern nation states. Yet, he loved the land that had nurtured him and never abandoned a basic anti-colonial stance. He simply did not want Indian patriots to imitate European nationalists.

Tagore derived "immense pleasure in discovering India in Bali". However, he was deeply disturbed when the news reached about the publication of Katherine Mayo's book, *Mother India*. The book was hailed by pro-imperialist sections in different parts of the world because its objective was to prove that Indians were incapable of governing themselves. It may be recalled that Gandhiji, after reading the book, rightly characterized it as a "drainage inspector's report". Rabindranath Tagore wrote a denunciation of the book and sent it for publication to the *Manchester Guardian*.

Tagore discovered that the Hindu way of life provided sustenance to Bali, but it had its own unique characteristics. One incident mentioned by Prof. Sugata Bose is worth repeating. Tagore was accompanied by the Balinese king on his visits to different parts of Bali. One day, they saw a river flowing down the mountain. The king immediately chanted, "Ganga, *Jamuna, Narmada, Godavari. Kaveri, Saraswati*". These rivers in the north and south of India provided cultural unity to India. That concept of unity "had crossed the eastern oceans to reach distant islands". Tagore also noted that the King did not mention the river Indus, five rivers of the Punjab and the Brahmaputra. Tagore concluded that "these rives were not culturally part of ancient India" that had spread its influence across the Bay of Bengal at a particular moment in history.

Tagore was keen to interact with Indonesian educationists and visited a few educational institutions, which had similar aims as the Visva Bharati. Dewantoro had started the *Taman Sisva* (Garden of schools) and Tagore familiarized himself with their functioning. His visit led to the exchange of scholars and artists. The popularization of Batik was due to Javanese artists who came to India following Tagore's visit. As Prof. Arun Das Gupta has written, today "Tagore is hardly remembered as the first person to launch a cultural exchange programme. Nonetheless, he was a pioneer bridge-builder between India and Indonesia in our period".

In Bandung there was an unscheduled meeting between Tagore and Sukarno. With no Dutch officials present, conversation went on smoothly. Sukarno could speak English; he was accompanied by two young Sundanese nationalists. Tagore was happy to note that Sukarno was keeping abreast with Indian national movement and was familiar with Gandhi, Chittaranjan Das, Motilal Nehru and Sarojini Naidu. The poet was "charmed" by the young leader.

Hinduism in Indonesia

The Government of Indonesia has accorded Hinduism the status of official religion. The other official religions are Islam, Portestantism, Catholicism, Buddhism and Confucianism. The Hindus constitute 1.7 per cent of the total population and they number approximately 4 million. They are mainly concentrated in the Island of Bali, where they constitute 83.5 per cent of the population. What is more heartening there is no restriction on the practice of Hinduism.

❑

4

Indian Solidarity with Indonesia – Nationalist Phase

India championing the cause of Indonesian independence was a logical corollary of the manner in which the Indian national movement developed in the 19th and 20th centuries. The Indian National Congress, the main institutional expression of Indian nationalist aspirations, evinced keen interest in matters relating to foreign policy since its very inception. Though, in the initial stages, it was confined to resolutions in the annual sessions of the Congress, it became more pronounced with Mahatma Gandhi and Jawaharlal Nehru playing a dominant role in national politics. Gandhiji took a global view of the Indian nationalist movement. To quote Gandhiji:

> India is the key to the exploitation of the Asiatic and other non-European races on earth. She is held under bondage not merely for the sake of her own exploitation, but that of her neighbours, near and distant.

Gandhiji, therefore, appealed to Indians that they had a duty not only to free India, but the world from colonial oppression. To quote Gandhiji, again:

> My ambition is much higher than independence. Through the deliverance

> of India, I seek to deliver the so-called weaker races of the earth from the crushing heels of Western exploitation in which England is the greatest partner.

Nehru's Contribution

The Indian nationalist horizon widened and interest in international affairs became more intense with Jawaharlal Nehru becoming the "acknowledged spokesman" on foreign affairs. Nehru's philosophy of life cannot be explained easily. As his daughter Indira Gandhi, has summed up:

> He drew much from the thought of the East and the West and from the philosophies of the past and the present. Never religious in the formal sense, yet he had a deep love for the culture and tradition of his own land. Never a rigid Marxist, yet he was deeply influenced by that theory and was particularly impressed by what he saw in the Soviet Union on his first visit in 1927. However, he realized that the world was too complex and man had too many facets to be encompassed by any single or total explanation. He himself was a socialist with abhorrence for regimentation and a democrat who was conscious to reconcile his faith in civil liberty with the necessity of mitigating economic and social backwardness. His thoughts, both within himself and the outside world, to adjust such seeming contradictions are what make his life and work significant and fascinating.

Through his speeches and writings, Nehru influenced the Indian National Congress to pay greater attention to international affairs. Nehru underlined the need for a reorientation of the Indian outlook on world affairs and was mainly instrumental in making the Indian National Congress take a clear-cut stand on issues relating to freedom from colonial domination, and the necessity to fight against Fascism and Nazism. As his well-known biographer Sarvepalli Gopal has written:

> Jawaharlal Nehru played a decisive role in the history of the twentieth century – as a leader of the Indian people, as a representative of the new mood in Asia, and as a spokesman of the international conscience.

A study of Indian nationalist view of world affairs before independence gives a clue to the understanding of the main elements of Indian foreign policy, more especially its active role in furtherance of Indonesian independence. The main element undoubtedly had been the consistent support to the demand for independence of the colonial peoples. Equally important and, allied with it, had been the desire to keep India out of great power rivalry. In fact, in the first session of the Indian National Congress in 1885, a resolution was passed condemning the annexation of Upper Burma to British Empire. In later years, the Indian National Congress repeatedly condemned the use of Indian soldiers and resources in wars across Indian frontiers to serve British imperialist interests. Although the Indian National Congress supported the British Government during the First World War, hoping that such a move would hasten India's progress towards independence, it opposed the British during the Second World War in view of British reluctance to assure Indian independence. The freedom of dependant peoples and aversion to power politics of European powers were the two main elements of Indian nationalist view of world affairs.

Congress of the Oppressed Nationalities in Brussels, 1927

The international perspective further crystallised with participation in international conferences on the exploited and oppressed peoples. In February 1927, Jawaharlal Nehru attended the Congress of the Oppressed Nationalities in Brussels as the representative of the Indian National Congress. The Congress was the first of its kind and was attended by 174 delegates from 31 countries. The chief organizer was Willie Muenzenberg, German leader and head of the Communist International. The distinguished delegates, among others, included Henri Barbusse, French novelist and member of the French Communist Party; George Lansbury, leader of the British Labour Party; Ellen Wilkinson, leader of the British Labour Party; Fenner Brockway, British anti-war activist; Harry Pollitt, leader of the British Communist Party and active trade unionist; Reginald Bridgman, British diplomat; Ernst Toller, German playwright; Mohammad Hatta, Indonesian nationalist and Ho Chih Minh, leader of the Vietnamese nationalist movement.

The Brussels Conference, Jawaharlal Nehru has pointed out, was "an event of first class importance" and is "likely to have far reaching results". In Brussels, for the first time, as Iqbal Singh has written, Nehru came into contact with three political streams, 1) The European Socialist movement; 2) Asian, Latin American and nascent African nationalist movements; and 3) Marxist movements "in all its innocence and apocalyptic expectancy of the imminent collapse of capitalism and dawn of socialist millennium". One significant fall out was the recognition of the Indian National Congress by the progressive forces in the world as the "authentic voice of the Indian people".

In a statement to the press on 9 February 1927, Nehru pointed out that there was "much in common" in the struggles of "various subject and oppressed peoples". Their opponents, Nehru said, "are often the same, although they sometimes appear in different guises and the means employed for their subjection are often similar". He appealed for "greater contacts" and "closer co-operation" among the nationalists fighting for freedom. In a moving speech to the Congress on 10 February, Nehru attacked British imperialism for its exploitation and underlined the necessity to forge close links among Asian nationalists. Nehru pointed out that India was the key to the exploitation of Asia and that the freedom of India was essential pre-requisite for the emancipation of mankind. To quote Nehru:

> It is important for you if we win freedom. Not only internal freedom, but also freedom to make contacts with neighbours and other lands as we wish.

Nehru also expressed his shame in the use of the Indian troops by the British imperialists to oppress the peoples of China, Egypt, Mesopotamia, Tibet, Burma and other countries.

Indonesian Delegation

Nehru was impressed with the Indonesian delegation, which consisted of Hatta, Semaun, Nasir Pamuntjak and

Subardjo. In his report to the All India Congress Committee, Nehru said:

> The Indonesians, chiefly from Java, were even more interesting. They were Muslims, but even their names are partly derived from Sanskrit. Their customs, they told us, were still largely Hindu in origin, and many of them have a striking resemblance to the higher caste Hindus.

The contacts, which were established in Brussels, became very useful in later years in forging closer links with Asian countries, especially with Indonesia. Unfortunately the Congress of Oppressed Nationalities came under communist domination, and Nehru and Hatta were expelled from the League against Imperialism and National Independence as "national reformers". A few years later, in an address to the Indian Council of World Affairs, while reminiscing about the contacts with Indonesian nationalists, Nehru pointed out:

> We used to correspond sometimes and it might interest you to know that some of the friends that I met twenty years ago in the conference are running the Indonesian Republic today. And these contacts have stood as well now, because apart from knowing each other distantly, personal relationships made me personally more interested in Indonesia and, to a small extent, made them more interested in India.

Jawaharlal Nehru's relations with Mohammad Hatta

became intimate when Hatta became the Prime Minister of Indonesia in 1948. On his return from a state visit to Indonesia in 1950, Nehru wrote a letter of thanks to Mohammad Hatta. Nehru referred to him as his "oldest friend in Indonesia" and how his interest in Indonesian freedom "dates back to that time".

Establishment of Foreign Affairs Department

The Indian interest in international affairs was further heightened when the Indian National Congress established a separate Foreign Affairs Department in May 1935 under the direction of Jawaharlal Nehru. The Foreign Affairs Department became the training ground for many Indian nationalist leaders like Dr. Ram Manohar Lohia and Acharya Kripalani and was also the crucible in which many new ideas were tested and perfected. The Foreign Affairs Department can rightly be characterized as the precursor to the Ministry of External Affairs of independent India.

Nehru's understanding of world history and inter-relationship between Indian nationalism and developments across the world influenced Congress thinking. His famous statement that the gates of Indian freedom are to be found in Madrid on one hand and Chungking on the other was a reflection of how changing times had influenced Indian understanding of international affairs. As Prof. S. Gopal has mentioned Madrid was the "besieged capital of the Spanish civil war "and Chungking "was the symbol of the Chinese people, under the joint leadership of the Kuomintang and the Chinese Communist Party, fighting the ravages of Japanese militarism".

Shadow of Second World War

With the dark clouds of the Second World War gathering over the horizon, the Indian National Congress was naturally concerned with the momentous changes taking place in Southeast Asia. The rapid victory of Japan and the collapse of the imperialist forces, the mobilization of the Indian communities in the region under the banner of the Indian National Army, and the rapid march of the Japanese army, overrunning Andaman and Nicobar Islands and knocking at the doors of India sent shock waves throughout the country. In December 1941, the Congress Working Committee expressed its deep sympathy with the peoples of Burma, Malaya and East Indies in the trials and hardships that they were facing as a result of conflict among imperialist powers. In August 1942, when the Quit India resolution was adopted, Congress did not forget the Asian comrades and expressed its conviction that the "freedom of India must be the symbol of, and prelude to, the freedom of all other Asiatic nations under foreign domination".

How close the people of Indonesia were to Nehru's heart becomes evident if one reads through his speeches and writings during this period. The Selected Works of Jawaharlal Nehru contains the "stray notes" scribbled by Jawaharlal Nehru as reference material for his speech in the Congress Working Committee meeting on 5 August 1942. The first country to figure in the notes was Indonesia, to be followed by Korea, Ceylon and Nepal under the broad heading "zero hour of the world".

In the international conference of the Institute of Pacific Relations in 1945, Mrs. Vijaya Lakshmi Pandit pointed out that the days of imperialism were over and called for the independence of India, Burma, Indo-China and the East Indies. On 4 May 1945, Mrs. Pandit submitted a memorandum in the San Francisco Conference demanding independence for India and other Asiatic peoples. The Memorandum stated:

> I speak, in particular, for Burma, Malaya, Indo-China and Dutch East Indies, all bound to my own country by the closest ties of historical and cultural kinship and which cherish aspirations to national freedom like our own. Liberation from Japan would mean for them liberation from alien imperialism so far as this Conference is concerned.

Nehru's Visit to Malaya and Singapore

In 1946, Jawaharlal Nehru visited Malaya and Singapore to extend his sympathy and support to the people of Indian origin who suffered humiliation and suffering during the Second World War. He assured them that when India became independent, it will be able to "contribute its share to unite Asia and preserve peace in the world". In a speech in Singapore on 18 March, 1946 Nehru highlighted:

> The independence that India wants is not merely for herself. You cannot have the world half-free and half-slave. If India aspires for freedom, it is for a free world, and when India is free, every ounce of its energy shall be used for the freedom of all subject countries. This is true of Indonesia, Malaya or any other country in the world.

In a special article dated 3 March 1946, written in the *New York Times*, Jawaharlal Nehru made a special mention of the Indonesian struggle for freedom. To quote from this article:

In Indonesia we have been witnessing a clear case of shattered imperialism trying to hold on with the help of another imperialist power. Here is a country, well capable of looking after herself, with a functioning government which has obviously the support of the mass of the people, where there would certainly be peace and security if outsiders did not intervene.

❑

5

Glimpses into Indonesian Nationalism

One of the most significant political developments of the twentieth century is the national self-assertion and independence of Afro-Asian peoples. The First World War shattered the land empires in Europe; the Second World War struck a death blow to imperialist possessions in Asia. The movement soon gathered momentum and spread to the counties of the African continent.

Majority of colonies were pluralistic societies and, on independence, they were confronted with the problem of national integration. Indonesia, thanks to the genius of Sukarno, started to tackle these problems even when it was fighting for independence. Sukarno not only articulated the hopes and aspirations of his people, he also wanted them to forget their regional identities as Javanese, Ambonese, Minangkabaus and Makkasarese and think themselves as Indonesians. The geographical limits of the country were spelt out, when Sukarno used to frequently refer to Indonesia as one stretching from Sabang (northern tip of Sumatra) to Merauke (in Papua New Guinea). He used to speak about the greatness of Indonesia during the Majapahit period and effectively used history as a tool to unify his people. Equally significant, the nationalist leaders used to communicate with people in *Bahasa* Indonesia; on the attainment of independence, it was adopted as the national and official language of the country, without any controversy, Sukarno imagined Indonesia, long before Benedict Anderson publicized the concept of "imagined communities".

The Indonesian archipelago is a sprawling chain of more than 17, 800 islands stretching from the southern tip of the Nicobar Islands to the shores of Australia. It was the lure of the fabled spices of the Indies, which brought the European merchants to these islands in the sixteenth century. In the bitter struggle for the monopoly of spice trade, the Dutch East India Company had the complete backing of the Government and its armed forces; gradually, the Company began to control the external trade. In 1798, the Dutch East India Company collapsed and the Netherlands Government assumed direct control.

With the Indonesian society politically fragmented, the Dutch found it easy to extend their control throughout the archipelago. By 1910, the process was complete. The contribution of East Indies to the prosperity of Holland was immeasurable. The Dutch Governor General Van den Bosch wrote: "It is certain that without the generous contribution of the Indies, the State would have been ruined and we would have been forced to submit ourselves to the mercy of the opposition". The well known historian of the colonial period, J. S. Furnivall, has quoted a colonial master: "Java poured forth riches upon riches on the homeland as if by a magician's wand".

This chapter does not provide an exhaustive analysis of Indonesian nationalist movement. I have touched upon important milestones and have highlighted parallels between India and Indonesia.

Boedi Utomo (Noble Endeavour)

A small group of Javanese intellectuals founded an organisation called *Boedi Utomo* (Noble Endeavour) on 30

May 1908. It was established by a retired Javanese doctor named Wahidin Soediraoesada, with the support of few social reformers. It was a social and cultural organization and did not have much impact on Dutch administration. However, historians trace the beginnings of Indonesian nationalism to *Boedi Utomo*. During the freedom movement 30 May was celebrated as the National Awakening Day.

Sarekat Islam

Four years later, in 1912, another organization called *Sarekat Islam* (Islamic Association) was formed. It was an association of Javanese traders who were concerned with the entry of Chinese merchants into the Batik industry. It was quickly transformed into a mass political organization by Umar Syed Tjokroaminoto. In 1917 the party proclaimed independence as its goal. By 1919 it had a membership of one and a half million. Gradually the communists penetrated into the organization and factionalism developed within it. Gradually the influence of *Sarekat islam* began to decline.

Indonesian Nationalist Party (P.N.I.)

The founding of the Indonesian Nationalist Party (P.N.I.) in 1927 marks an important milestone in the development of Indonesian nationalism. Under the dynamic leadership of Sukarno, the P.N.I. united all the anti-imperialist forces under its banner and took an uncompromising stand on independence and rejected any form of co-operation with the Dutch. Sukarno, the founder of the P.N.I., like Gandhi, was a product of evolution. Many influences fashioned his life. Of these, Indian influences had been very profound. Born of a Javanese father and Balinese mother in 1901, the young Kusno imbibed the Hinduised Javanese culture through the world of *Wajang*.

He listened and watched with awe and admiration the stories and performances of the *Wajang* heroes – Arjuna, Bhima, Gatotkacha, Indra, Hanuman and a host of others - each with his own noble characteristics. In his childhood, as Bernard Dahm points out in his book, *Sukarno and the Struggle for Indonesian Independence*, it was with Bhima that Sukarno tried to identify himself. The stories of the Ramayana and Mahabharata provided abundant opportunities for the Dalang to express the innermost political aspirations in a language and manner easily understood by the people. Night after night, as the young Kusno watched the *Wajang*, the desire for independence slowly filled his mind. More often than not, he considered himself as the *Dalang* "shaping the events of this universe and expounding their inner meaning".

As a student, Sukarno was also introduced to Theosophy by his father and became familiar with the writings of Annie Besant, who became the President of the Indian National Congress. Like Gandhiji, who experienced racial segregation in South Africa, Sukarno was made aware of the colonial caste system prevailing in European elementary school in Surabaya. After frequent humiliations, he decided to fight it; he felt the pride and self-confidence of a free man and tried to instill the same feelings among his contemporaries. Self-help, self-reliance and self-confidence – these concepts became the bywords of his political philosophy.

Sukarno had his political apprenticeship in Tjokroaminoto's house, where he met Islamic scholars, secular nationalists and Marxist intellectuals. He believed that if there was no unity among them, the Dutch rule would indefinitely continue in Indonesia. His political programme was directed to the unity of all nationalist forces and in pinpointing those elements of the struggle where unity could be accomplished. Like Gandhi, he believed in converting the nationalist movement into a mass movement. He passionately subscribed to mass politics and mass organizations. Though he was influenced by Marxist ideals, like Gandhi again, he felt that the Marxist concept of the proletariat had no relevance to Asian agrarian societies and developed his own concept of *Marhaenism*.

Marhaen is a childhood acquaintance of Sukarno. He was an ordinary peasant, owning a small plot of land, living in Bandung. His experience with life constitutes the bedrock of *Marhaenism*. *Marhaen* can be a peasant, a petty trader, a labourer, a fisherman or a peddler. Sukarno propounded the view that the anti-colonialist struggle in Indonesia should not be based on class conflict but on the unity of all sections of population.

In order to unify the scattered anti-imperialist forces, Sukarno propounded a new and dynamic concept of nationalism. In the development of this nationalist philosophy, Sukarno was influenced by the writings of Renan, Wells, Marx, Engels, Sun Yat Sen and Gandhi. Sukarno condemned the exclusiveness and chauvinism of European nationalism and asserted that his nationalism was based on the love of all humanity. Quoting Gandhi, Sukarno said:

> My love of the homeland is part of
> my love of all mankind. I am a patriot
> because I am a man and a human being.
> No one is excluded from my love.

This feeling, Sukarno said, was the secret that had given Gandhi the power to unite the Hindus, Muslims, Parsis, Jains and Sikhs. He quoted Chittaranjan Das to explain the characteristics of Western imperialism. To quote:

> European nationalism has an aggressive character, is a nationalism which is concerned with its own needs, a commercial nationalism that can lead to profit or loss, but that in the end must perish or be destroyed.

Sukarno successfully used the slogan of nationalism to unite the forces of Islam, secular nationalism and Marxism, which were hitherto working at cross purposes. He frequently used the example of the Indian national movement, to the "indissoluble union" between nationalist Gandhi and the pan – Islamists – Maulana Mohammad Ali and Shaukat Ali, to drive home his point.

Perihmpunan Indonesia

Indonesian students studying in Holland were influenced by radical nationalism sweeping across Europe. They formed the *Perihmpunan Indonesia* in 1922. It was the first organization to refer to their motherland as Indonesia. Its mouthpiece was called *Indonesia Merdeka* (Indonesian freedom). The *Perihmpunan Indonesia* advocated complete non-cooperation with the Dutch Government. The most important leader of *Perihmpunan Indonesia* was Mohammad Hatta. As mentioned earlier, he participated in the Congress of Oppressed Nationalities in Brussels in 1927 as Indonesian representative.

Pan Asianism

The Indonesian nationalist triumvirate viewed their struggle as an integral part of the wider Asian struggle for freedom from imperialist domination and the establishment of an egalitarian society. They have repeatedly stated that they admired and also derived great inspiration from India's struggle for freedom. As Sukarno put it:

> Just as we are your debtors in culture, so too are we your debtors in political faith. Since 1908, we have given no little attention to your aspirations and political movements. Dadabhai Naoroji, Sunrendranath Bannerjee, Gopal Krishna Gokhale, Aurobindo, Bal Gangadhar Tilak, Lajpat Rai, Dr. Ansari and Dr. Abdul Kalam Azad are honoured names. And Mahatma Gandhi and Jawaharlal Nehru are names to conjure with in Indonesia.

Sukarno's favourite quotation was Swami Vivekananda's exhortation, "Awake, Arise, Stop not till the goal is reached".

Indonesia Accuses

The speeches and writings of Sukarno were circulated widely and his popularity increased by leaps and bounds. The decline of *Sarekat Islam*, the failure of the left following the abortive attempt to capture power in 1927 and political stirrings among Indonesian students studying in European Universities - all these developments contributed to the creation of a new political landscape. The "new nationalism" spelt out by Sukarno sprouted on a fertile soil. The Dutch Government, perturbed by Sukarno's popularity, detained him in 1929.

Sukarno was an astute politician and converted his trial by the court into an opportunity. His defence published as Indonesia Accuses, is a testament of his faith. It reflected his thorough grasp of the inter-relationship between imperialism and capitalism and his extensive reading on the subject. Parallels with national movements sweeping across different parts of the world were alluded to. He had abiding faith that the logic of history would lead to the eventual downfall of the Dutch empire. Sukarno concluded his oration with the following words:

> There is no people who can attain greatness without national independence; there is no country that can be firm and strong without being free. Conversely, no colony can attain glory; no colony can attain greatness. Therefore, every colonial people desire freedom so that it can attain greatness. Every people who lack freedom, every people which because of that is unable to control its own affairs, in its own interests and for its own happiness, live in an unsettled atmosphere.

Sukarno was confident that despite the bravado displayed by the colonialists, the logic of history would lead to their eventual downfall. Sukarno said, "The sun does not rise because the cock crows; the cock crows because the sun rises".

From an Indian point of view, it should be mentioned that Sukarno's defence oration contained many references to the genesis and growth of the Indian national movement. History, Sukarno said, "is the story of human peoples or nations trying to escape misfortune" and alluded to several examples starting from the sufferings of Jesus Christ to the Chinese and Indian resistance against imperialism. In this connection he referred to the "Indian people led by Tilak and Gandhi opposing the foreign greed". He quoted from Sarojini Naidu's presidential address in the annual session of the Indian National Congress held in Kanpur in 1925 to substantiate his conviction that the indomitable spirit would surmount all difficulties. To quote:

> Who can enchain a people if their spirit will not be enchained who can destroy a people if their spirit will not be destroyed

In his concluding remarks, Sukarno cited the speech made by Lokamanya Bal Gangadhar Tilak in the Bombay High Court in 1909:

> It may be the will of providence that the cause which I represent is to prosper more by my suffering than by my remaining free.

Summing up the profound influence of Indian national movement on Indonesia, Khoo Kay Hock has highlighted:

> The Indian nationalist struggle was followed closely by the Indonesian nationalists. The *Boedi Utomo*, for instance, looked to India to obtain teachers in their educational programme. Its members regarded Tagore and Gandhi as great national leaders. The non-cooperation policy and passive resistance tactics of Gandhi were copied by *Partai Nasional Indonesia* and *Partindo* in the later stages when early confidence in Dutch good intentions gave way to militancy and anti-Dutch sentiment.

Sukarno Analyses India's Weakness

Under the Banner of Revolution, brought out by the Publication Committee, Jakarta contains an interesting article written by Sukarno in 1941. It provides a succinct answer to the claim made by Western writers that India is "not capable of governing itself". Sukarno raised the question: Can India build its defence strength? Sukarno wrote that strategically India is better placed than Germany or Japan. People of India are brave as is evident in the experience of the Sikhs, Marathas, Rajputs and the Gurkhas. But these brave people were defeated because of disunity among Indians themselves. In the Revolt of 1857, the British could have been defeated, had it not been for the support extended by the Sikhs to British rulers. Sukarno highlighted the military achievements of Samudra Gupta, Shivaji and Akbar. India will have to learn lessons from its history as to why it came under imperialist domination. Sukarno concluded the article with a quotation from the Presidential address given by Srinivasa Iyengar in the 1926 annual session of the Indian National Congress: "When India is free, India will be able to, and is sure to, build up and maintain an army and a navy that accords with the requirements of modern age".

Impact of Japanese Occupation

The Japanese Occupation (March 1942 - August 1945) hastened the independence of Indonesia. The harsh military rule, rising inflation, black market and rampant corruption and introduction of forced labour brought in its turn untold misery and suffering.

The official policy of Japan was to promote the slogan of "Asia for Asians". It was fully exploited by the Indonesian nationalists to promote their objectives. Sukarno returned to Java from exile, so also Hatta and Sjahrir, who were released from prison. They held detailed discussions with other nationalist leaders. After considerable deliberations, the nationalists decided to adopt a dual policy, one section would ostensibly co-operate with Japan while the other would carry on the resistance movement. Sukarno and Hatta officially sided with the Japanese, while the under-ground resistance was masterminded by Sutan Sjahrir, with the co-operation of Amir Sjarifuddin and Dipto Mangunkusumo.

The myth surrounding *Djoyoboyo* convinced the Javanese that Japanese occupation was a prelude to independence. *Djoyoboyo* was King of Kediri, who ruled in the 12th century. According to legend, it was prophesied that Java will be occupied by yellow skinned conquerors who will rule for the life time of a maize plant. When the maize ripened and was ready for harvest the conquerors would leave and Java would be free. The similarity with Japanese occupation was obvious.

In March 1943, Japan established the *Pusat Tenaga Rakyat or PUTERA*, Centre of People's Power, of which Sukarno was made the Chairman. *The PUTERA* brought various groups of nationalists together. In order to train a local army corps for the "defence of the Fatherland" the *Sakarela Tentera Penbela Yanah Air* or PETA came into existence. The Islamic groups – *Nahadatul Ulama, Muhammadiya* and *Partai Sarekat Islam* - came together and formed the *Masjumi*. Contrary to Japanese expectations, the organizations they sponsored turned out to be focal points of Indonesian nationalism. In 1943, Sukarno and his colleagues visited Japan to thank the government for associating the Indonesian nationalists with the war-time administration.

Was Sukarno a patriot or a collaborator? The debate will go on for a long time and it is unlikely a unanimous view will emerge. But the fact remains that Sukarno made the best of the situation. In a conversation with P.R.S Mani on his role during the Japanese Occupation, Sukarno used an analogy frequently used by Gandhiji. It was about *Hamsa Kshira*. If water and milk (*Kshira*) are mixed and kept before the *Hamsa* (mythical swan), it drinks only the milk and leaves aside the water. Sukarno did the same thing. And, what is more, he emerged as the only unifying force in the country at the end of the Second World War.

❑

6

Indonesia Proclaims Independence

The military fortunes of Japan began to take a turn for the worse from 1943. Japan became desperate and wanted to consolidate Indonesian support and made a promise of independence. A Preparatory Committee for Indonesian Independence was formed in January 1944. On 8 August 1945, Japan announced that independence would be granted on August 24, 1945. However, sections of radical Indonesian youth began to pressurize Sukarno to proclaim the independence of Indonesia without waiting for official Japanese proclamation. Then it was announced that Japan might surrender at any time. And if the surrender took place before August 24, Indonesia would be cheated of her independence. On August 15, the news came that Japan had surrendered.

Time was fast running out. After some hesitation, Sukarno and Hatta agreed with the radical elements and proclaimed the independence of Indonesia over radio on 17 August 1945. The Independence Preparatory Committee assembled the next day and elected Sukarno as the President and Hatta as the Vice-President. Sutan Sjahrir became the Prime Minister and, concurrently, was appointed as Minister for Foreign Affairs. A few days later, Sukarno and Hatta relinquished their executive authority, but retained their posts. The Indonesian Revolution had begun.

From its very inception, the infant Republic had to face the Dutch challenge. Holland was keen to restore its rule as early as possible over the archipelago. In order to thwart the Dutch plans, the Indonesian nationalists were keen to get international recognition of the Republic, which alone could prevent the restoration of the Dutch colonial power. Sukarno, Hatta and Sjahrir were convinced that international intervention on the side of the Republic was the need of the hour. As Michael Leifer has pointed out, securing "international recognition in order to deny the restoration of the colonial power " was the main objective of the foreign policy of Indonesian Republic. Armed resistance was inevitable, but what was more important, was the mobilization of international solidarity. Here the Indian role became the most important factor for the furtherance of Indonesian cause.

Indian Support

The momentous developments in Indonesia, following the declaration of independence, fired the imagination of Indian leaders. India spontaneously expressed its support to Indonesia. President Sukarno got in touch with the Indian leaders and invited Jawaharlal Nehru to visit Indonesia for an on-the-spot study of the situation. On 15 October 1945, Nehru not only welcomed the birth of the Indonesian Republic, he also urged the Indians to express their solidarity with the Indonesian Republic. On 23 October 1945, Nehru demanded that the British Government of India should recognise Sukarno's government immediately. Nehru, however, could not visit Indonesia, because the British Government refused to provide him the necessary facilities.

Nehru exhorted the Indian dock workers not to load any

war materials meant for the suppression of the Indonesian cause. He welcomed the initiative taken by the Australian and Chinese trade unions. In a letter addressed to Sardar Patel on 16 October 1945, Nehru gave expression to what sort of role India should play in this regard:

> The Indonesian struggle is becoming more intense and I feel that we ought to give it a greater prominence. It would be a good thing if there were meetings etc. But the most dramatic thing would be for our dock workers and sea men to refuse to load war materials for Java, as the Australians did.

Problems faced by Dock Workers

Jawaharlal Nehru was sensitive to the problems faced by the Indonesian dock workers who were stranded in India. Fired by Intense nationalism, Indonesian workers, working in ships berthed in India, resorted to non-co-operation. The ship owners immediately retrenched them. These workers had to be sent back to Indonesia. The Indonesian Students Committee in India took up their cause. In a letter to Jawaharlal Nehru, the Committee pointed out that these sea men "were bitter against the Dutch" because they were forcibly recruited to the Dutch Merchant Navy "without their consent". What is more, they genuinely felt that they "were not fighting for their country". Hence, they refused to work in the ships. Some of them got in touch with Mohammad Ali Jinnah and the Muslim League, but did not elicit even an iota of sympathy from them.

Nehru immediately took up their cause. In a letter to Yusuf Meharally, then Mayor of Bombay, Nehru pointed out that the Dutch Consulate in Bombay would not extend any help to the Indonesian workers. He, therefore, appealed to Meharally to look into their immediate problems relating to food and accommodation. Meharally sorted out the problems relating to day-to-day living. After the formation of the interim Government, New Delhi got in touch with concerned Republican authorities. Finally the Indonesian workers were sent back to Indonesia from Madras in the middle of June 1946 in a British ship Sunera.

Deployment of Indian Soldiers in Indonesia

The dominant thinking in the post-Second World War period was that the days of colonialism were over and the former colonies would be granted independence soon. The British decision to grant independence to India, Pakistan, Burma and Ceylon and the upsurge of nationalist feelings in many African countries created feelings of optimism.

The developments in Indonesia, however, cast a long shadow of despair over the prevailing sense of optimism. The determination of the Dutch to restore colonial rule, with open support from the Western World, had its inevitable fallout in the domestic politics of Indonesia. There were two schools of thought as to how the struggle should be followed. The first view subscribed to the efficacy of the diplomatic approach, a point of view advocated by the senior leaders, more especially the nationalist triumvirate. If the Republic could consolidate its power and project an image of reasonableness, it would lead to smooth transfer of power. The opposite view, the *Permuda* view, subscribed to *Perdjuangan* (struggle); it did not have any faith in the bona fide of the Dutch Government. What is more, the Dutch should be compelled to make concessions and these concessions could be extracted only through long and protracted struggle. The *Permuda* view was eloquently articulated by Tan Malaka and his revolutionary followers. In the final analysis, it was the diplomatic approach which succeeded, but, at the same time, it must be highlighted that the hands of the Indonesian leaders were strengthened by the many acts of heroism and bravery displayed by the revolutionaries in Surabaya, Bandung and other places.

The first formidable challenge, which faced the Indian nationalists, arose out of the British decision to deploy Indian soldiers to take the surrender of Japan and restore law and order. The Indian forces landed in Java on 29 September 1945. Unfortunately, the Indian forces clashed with the Indonesian nationalists in Surabaya, Bandung, Semerang, Ambarawa and other places. Mohammad Hatta brought these incidents to the notice of Jawaharlal Nehru. In a letter written on 1 December 1945, Hatta remarked:

> I do not know what will be the end of all this British provocative action. One thing is certain; it will not bring peace and order in Indonesia for which the British is supposed to be in Indonesia. Certainly, the British will finally break down the Indonesian armed resistance, but they cannot suppress the spirit of independence.

The Indian nationalists were convinced that the use of Indian troops was intended to restore Dutch colonialism in Indonesia. Naturally, the British decision aroused Indian indignation. Even before the dispatch of the Indian troops to Indonesia, the Indian National Congress made its stand clear. In a resolution passed in September 1945, the Congress declared:

> In particular, the AICC would take strong objection to the use of Indian troops in maintaining imperialist domination over any part of these countries of Southeast Asia or West Asia.

British Government did not pay any heed to Indian concerns and decided to collaborate with Dutch imperialists. Nehru became more indignant at the British action and said: "It was a matter of shame that the British Empire should be using all its might to establish a Dutch Empire in Indonesia". He warned the imperialist powers:

> The movement of the people of Indonesia for freedom cannot be suppressed by force. The fire of freedom which has been lit in Asia will not extinguish till it has consumed the whole imperialist machinery.

Indian Soldiers Join Indonesian Ranks

The sustained campaign undertaken by the Indian National Congress received warm support from all sections of Indian population. "Southeast Asia day" was observed throughout the country on 28 October 1945.

Indian opposition to the use of Indian troops in Indonesia had its fallout on the British Indian soldiers. P.R.S. Mani, in his monograph, quotes a Rajput soldier telling him in Surabaya, "Why should we die for the Dutch, Sir". The feeling that Indian soldiers should not be used for suppressing Indonesian nationalists began to gain ground. The consequence was that 700 of them deserted the British Army. Some of them were captured by the Allied forces and kept in detention in Sumatra under most unhygienic conditions. The more heroic among them joined the ranks of the Indonesian army and made invaluable contribution to the Indonesian struggle for freedom.

The British Commander took a legalist view and condemned the Indian soldiers as "deserters" and wanted maximum punishment to be given to them. On the other hand, Jawaharlal Nehru was determined to ensure that no action should be taken and they should safely return to India. Prime Minister Sjahrir concurred with Nehru's views; he felt that their case was "exceptional" as they were motivated by idealistic considerations. N. Raghavan, Consul General of India in Indonesia, took personal interest and visited the detention centres, spoke to the Indian soldiers and made arrangements with a British ship for their return to India. The Republican Government made a noble gesture by issuing a certificate to each one of the Indian soldiers. The certificate was signed by Mohammad Hatta, Vice- President of the Indonesian Republic. The certificate made a special mention of those soldiers, who sacrificed their lives for Indonesian freedom. Their graves "will be a symbol of friendship and unity between Indian and the Indonesian people".

Contributions of Indian Journalists

Indian journalists posted in Indonesia, T.G. Narayanan of the *Hindu* and P.R.S. Mani of the *Free Pres Journal*, through their dispatches, created awareness about Indonesia in India. Narayanan was senior to Mani in age. It was admiration at first sight. They were students of Madras Christian College. Both were passionately committed to Indonesian freedom. As mentioned earlier, Jawaharlal Nehru made use of their services to understand the crosscurrents of Southeast Asian politics, and in promoting India-Indonesia relations. The two journalists strengthened the legitimacy of the Indonesian Republic and exposed the machinations of the Dutch imperialists. Mani writes in his Monograph, *Look Up and Aim High*, that he used to personally carry Narayanan's comments on the Indian National Army and submit them to Sarat Chandra Bose in Calcutta "for onward transmission to Jawaharlal Nehru in Allahabad".

In a special article in the *Hindu*, dated 4 January 1946, Sukarno gave expression to his indebtedness to India. Two days later, Vice- President Mohammad Hatta also contributed an article, echoing the same feelings. I am quoting below from Sukarno's article:

> In the wide world around us, there are countless friends and well wishers who are aiding us with their moral support and active help. Among you, our brothers and comrades in India, there are hosts of sympathizers and helpers. Your workers have struck work as a gesture of solidarity. Your press is supporting our cause. Your great leader Nehru's utterances on behalf of our freedom have been a source of immense strength to us in our hour of trial and tribulation. How shall I ever be able to convey to you the deep stirring of emotion that wells in every one of us when we think of the wonderful manner in which you have rallied to our cause. Deep down his heart, every Indonesian utters a silent prayer, "God bless you, our brothers and friends in India".

Policy of the Interim Government

As long as India remained a British colonial possession, Indian nationalists could not do much beyond expressing solidarity. However, with the assumption of power of the Interim Government on 2 September 1946, the capacity of the Indian leaders to extend assistance to the freedom fighters of other Asian countries increased. In his first broadcast to the nation, as Vice-President of the Interim Government, Jawaharlal Nehru underlined the necessity to forge closer relations with Asian neighbours.

> We are of Asia and the peoples of Asia are nearer and closer to us than others. India is so situated that she is the pivot of Western, Southern and Southeast Asia. In the past her culture flowed to all these countries and they came to her in many ways. These contacts are being renewed and the future is bound to see a closer union between India and Southeast Asia on one side and Afghanistan, Iran and Arab world on the other. To the furtherance of that closer association of free countries, we must devote ourselves.

Nehru also reiterated that India would not spare any efforts to rid Asia of colonialism. In his first press conference, after assuming power in the Interim Government, Nehru said:

> India will watch with close interest the development of events in Palestine, Iran, Indonesia, China, Siam and Indo-China as well as foreign possessions in

> India, with every sympathy, with the aspirations of the people of other lands for the attainment of internal peace, freedom where they lack it, and their place in the community of nations.

The first foreign policy decision of the interim Government pertained to Indonesia. It decided to call back the Indian troops sent there to ensure the surrender of Japan. As mentioned earlier, these troops unfortunately clashed with the Republican army in few places. In the first press conference as Minister-in-Charge of Foreign Affairs and Commonwealth Relations, Nehru declared that the kernel of Indian foreign policy would be the end of colonialism all over Asia. Nehru said that, in practice, the interim Government recognized the Indonesian Republic. "We have one hundred per cent sympathy for them. We want them to win through and through and establish their freedom and we want to help them and support them in every way".

In his broadcast as the Vice-President of the Interim Government on 7 September 1946, Nehru underlined the necessity to forge close friendship and association among Asian countries. He made a special mention of the Indonesian struggle for independence and said, "India has followed with anxious interest the struggle of the Indonesians for freedom and to them we send out good wishes".

Indonesia – India Rice Agreement

Credit for the Indonesia-India Rice Agreement should go to P.R. S. Mani. In the course of a conversation with Sutan Sjahrir, then Prime Minister, in April 1946 Mani mentioned that India was facing acute shortage of food grains; he felt that Java, which produced enormous quantity of rice, with three crops a year, "could come to the assistance of India". Expressing his sympathy to the Indian people, Sjahrir offered half a million tons of rice. However, he wanted India to arrange ships for the export of rice. And, in return, India could send textiles and medicines, which were in short supply in Indonesia. Apart from consolidating the goodwill, Sjahrir realized that the arrival of ships from India would mean that the Dutch blockade of Republican territory was destined to failure. The Dutch blockade had adversely affected inter-island transport and also traditional barter trade between Indonesia and Singapore. The trade pact would also enhance the international legitimacy of the Indonesian Republic.

Indian nationalists were extremely happy with the Indonesian offer of rice. On 20 April 1946, Nehru sent a cable to Sjahrir:

> I have learnt through the press that you have been good enough to offer to send half a million tons of rice from Indonesia to India to relieve famine conditions here, provided the necessary shipping is arranged for. I also understand that you are in great need of textiles from India...Half a million tons of rice or other food grains would make a great difference to India in the months to come.

The task of galvanizing the people behind the Government's rice offer was entrusted to Vice-President Mohmmad Hatta. In a nation- wide broadcast on 22 June 1946, Hatta declared that rice offer was based on humanitarianism, one of the basic principles of Indonesian nationalism. Despite the obstructions put by the Dutch authorities at every stage, the deal was carried through. The Indian Government arranged the ships in Singapore; on 27 July 1946, the Food Secretary to the Government of India signed and exchanged the Agreement with Prime Minister Sjahrir. The Agreement was signed even before the formation of the Interim Government. Nehru used his personal clout with the British Government to ensure that the rice deal went through without a hitch. In a cable to the Colonial Secretary, Nehru requested the British Government to overrule military objections. According to Mani, Indonesia was able to fulfill most part of the stipulated supply of rice to India and received in return agricultural implements, textiles, medicines and miscellaneous goods required by the people.

First Anniversary of the Indonesian Republic

It was a good omen that the first anniversary of the proclamation of Indonesian independence immediately followed the implementation of the Rice Agreement. The "constructive co-operation", as Sjahrir termed it, between the two countries had begun and it held forth the promise of a bright future. For Mani it was a vindication of a "scoop" which many commentators felt was unrealistic. So great was the camaraderie that, as mentioned earlier, the Republican flag and the Congress tricolor were hoisted by the President. In his address to the nation, Sukarno made a special mention of the growing friendship between the two countries. A couple of days later, Sukarno wrote a personal letter to Jawaharlal Nehru thanking him for his efforts in making the world aware of the "Indonesian question". After describing the age-old "ties of blood and culture" between the two countries, Sukarno added:

Flags of Indian National Congress and Indonesian Republic

We can never sufficiently thank you. Indonesians can never forget what you yourself or what India has done for us. Ingratitude is not one of our sins. We shall always cherish the help and goodwill we have received from you and we look forward to fruitful and friendly co-operation.

❑

7

India – Window to the Outside World

India's policy towards Indonesia, on the eve of independence, represented both continuity and change. Mention has already been made that during the nationalist movement, the Indian leaders considered the Indonesian struggle for freedom as an integral part of India's fight for independence. Nehru declared that the "kernel" of India's foreign policy was to get rid of colonialism from Asia at the earliest. With the formation of the Interim Government, Indian policy makers realized that idealism had to be combined with existing realities in the global scene. This stance will become evident in subsequent sections.

In his lucidly written book, *Beyond Autonomy: Indian Foreign Policy*, academic-turned diplomat A.K. Damodaran has pointed out that the "dominant motivation" of Indian nationalism was the "search for total autonomy in decision making". India has to find its place in the comity of nations by responding to new challenges and opportunities. It has to be done within the overarching framework of genuine sovereignty "buttressed by true democracy and the pluralistic version of secularism".

I want to illustrate the conflict between idealism and realism with an example. Nehru spoke, in a spirit of euphoria, on 9 August 1947, six days before independence, about the need for a Monroe Doctrine for Asia. The statement was made in the backdrop of continuing Dutch intransigence in Indonesia. Citing American example, Nehru said:

> The doctrine expounded by President Monroe had saved America from foreign aggression for nearly a hundred years and now the time has come when a similar doctrine has to be expounded with respect to Asian countries.

With the benefit of hindsight, it could definitely be stated that the idea was completely unrealistic. There was no unity among Asian countries and they inevitably got drawn into the Cold War. In the Afro-Asian Conference in Bandung in 1955, there were under-currents of hostility and mutual recrimination. Similarly, India-China friendship, which was the bedrock of India's Southeast Asia policy, during the 1950's, could not be sustained because Sino-Indian friendship got frozen in the snows of the Himalayas. After the 1962 military debacle, Nehru admitted that India was living "in an artificial world of our own creation". As Ambassador Jagat Mehta has pointed out, Nehru "did not anticipate a belligerent China would destroy the illusion of peace as the priority among the new nations of Asia". The Chinese betrayal shattered Nehru and hastened his death.

Full Story yet to be Told

P.R.S. Mani, who was deeply involved in Indonesia, in his Monograph, *The Story of Indonesian Revolution*, has pointed out that the "full story is yet to be told". To quote Mani:

> In the classified archives of the Government of India, there is a memorandum still to be released for publication, which gives the totality of

> the entire spectrum of aid given to the Indonesian Republic. Till its release, suffice it to say, that no request of the Republic went unheeded at the hands of Nehru.

Window to the Outside World

The first objective of Sjahrir, Foreign Minister of the Republic of Indonesia, was to get international recognition and support to the infant Republic. Since India, during those years, was Indonesia's closest ally, the Indonesian Republic opened an office in New Delhi. It was located in 1, Aurangazeb Road. Dr. Soedarsono was chosen to represent Indonesia. A medical doctor by profession, Soedarsono actively participated in the Indonesian nationalist movement. He also shared the ideas and ideals of the nationalist triumvirate.

The Indonesian Office faced number of problems in its day-to-day functioning. The most important among them was the shortage of finance. Understanding the predicament, Indian foreign office used to occasionally extend financial aid. Another source of finance for the Indonesian Embassy was the sale proceeds of rice given to India, which amounted to Rs 1,800,000/-. Gradually, the Indonesian office in New Delhi began to expand its activities to neigbouring countries. On one occasion, running short of finance, Dr. Soedarsono wrote a letter to Jawaharlal Nehru requesting for a loan of Rs. 300, 000/-. A perusal of the relevant papers indicates that there was objection from senior officials in the Finance Ministry. The Finance Ministry was not in favour of a loan to a foreign mission; what is more, the conservative senior officials felt that it will turn out to be a "bad debt". Jawaharlal Nehru intervened and, finally, the grant was made available from the secret funds of the Government of India.

Financial assistance to Indonesia became a good precedent and, in subsequent years, New Delhi provided substantial support to the African National Congress (A.N.C.) and the Palestine Liberation Organisation (P.L.O.), including much needed finance. Senior officials in the Ministry of External Affairs told me that such a gesture was in conformity with the greater objectives of expressing India's solidarity with South Africans in their struggle against apartheid and the struggle of the Palestinians against a Zionist state.

Asian Relations Conference, March-April 1947

Indian attempts to foster unity and co-operation among Asian countries reached its zenith in March-April 1947, when India, still under foreign domination, took the initiative and convened the Asian Relations Conference in New Delhi. Dr. Gopal has highlighted its significance succinctly: "For ten days from 23 March to 2 April, Delhi saw itself as the natural centre of a resurgent continent, conscious of its glorious past and forging links for the future".

The Conference was not official in character in that it was sponsored not by the Interim Government, but by the Indian Council of World Affairs, a non-political organization devoted to the study of international relations and India's role in it. However, the brain behind the Conference was Jawaharlal Nehru, who, to quote Prof. Appadorai, Secretary of the Asian Relations Conference, "provided every assistance that the Indian Council of World Affairs asked for". The Conference was attended by representatives of twenty-eight countries, including Soviet Central Asia. The delegates represented more than half of the world's population.

The Indonesian leaders were very happy because it was the first International Conference in which they were participating. Jawaharlal Nehru was very keen that Dr. Sjahrir should lead the Indonesian delegation, but Dr. Sjahrir was busy with negotiations leading to the Linggadjati Agreement. He could come to New Delhi only during the final stages of the Conference. The Indonesian all-party delegation, therefore, was led by Dr. Abu Hanifa, the leader of the *Masjumi*. The list of members read like a who's who in Indonesia. The Indonesian delegation was the largest in the Conference; it consisted of twenty five delegates and six observers.

Abu Hanifa, after his introauctory remarks, read out the message sent by Dr. Sjahrir. The message stated:

> The Indonesian Republic and the people of Indonesia accord warm support to the aims and objects underlying the organization of this conference. We trust that it will have a far-reaching influence in bringing together the governments and peoples of all Asian countries.

The idea of the Conference was in the air for several months. Jawaharlal Nehru discussed the idea with several colleagues and they concurred with his view. As Nehru explained in the inaugural session:

> It so happened that we in India convened the Conference, but the idea of such a Conference arose simultaneously in many minds and in many countries of Asia. There was a widespread urge and

> an awareness that the time has come for us, peoples of Asia, to meet together, to hold together, and to advance together.

Nehru with Sjahrir

Nehru set the tone of the Conference in his inaugural address on 23 March 1947. He commenced his speech by posing a question, "What has brought you, men and women of Asia, to India? Why have you come from various countries of this mother continent of ours and gathered together in this ancient city of Delhi?" Providing an answer himself, Nehru clarified that it was some deeper urge that brought the Asian nationalists together. Asia, which was under imperialist domination for long, was preparing to play its role in world affairs and the Conference was the first in that direction. "In this crisis in world history", Nehru said, "Asia will play a vital role. The countries of Asia can no longer be used as pawns by others. They are bound to have their own policies in world affairs". He further declared that there would be no world peace unless "Asia was free and played her part".

Indonesian Question

The Indonesian question was one of the key issues discussed under "national movements for freedom" Indonesian delegates gave a detailed account of their struggle and the obstacles faced by the fledgling Indonesian Republic. They claimed that the Republic was "sovereign and free" in political, economic and cultural matters. Sjahrir had gone to Holland for negotiations with the Dutch Government. They emphasized that their leaders were not taking orders from the Dutch Government

Intervening in the debate, Jawaharlal Nehru made a specific mention about the presence of Indian troops in Indonesia soon after the culmination of the Second World War. The Indian nationalists, on several occasions, had strongly condemned the use of Indian soldiers to stifle Indonesian freedom. Nehru added that the first decision of the Interim Government was to order the withdrawal of British Indian forces from Indonesia. Because of logistical reasons, like the non-availability of sufficient ships, the withdrawal could be completed only by November 1946.

On his arrival in New Delhi, Sjahrir was given a rousing welcome. Extending a special welcome, Nehru said, "Indonesia has been playing such an important role in Asian and world events in recent years and the coming of Sjahrir is of considerable significance for our Conference and for us in India". In the course of his reply, Sjahrir responded:

> Our being here in large numbers is in fact due not only to our immense interest in what is happening here, but also due to the fact that we have been isolated for many years. We thought it should be a great thing if as many people as could be spared from our

> country could take advantage of such a splendid opportunity to meet so many representatives of nearly all Asia. That is why Indonesia is so greatly represented in the Conference.

The Indian delegates repeatedly stressed that India based its freedom movement on a wide concept of nationalism. The freedom of India was meaningless without the freedom of the oppressed people all over the world India's heart was not only with Indonesia in their struggle, but behind all those who desired freedom.

The Indonesian delegation was happy with the proceedings of the Conference. In a broadcast over All India Radio, Dr. Sjahrir expressed confidence:

> We in Asia have now got together for the first time. Let us then set to work together in real earnest for the benefit of all mankind and we shall certainly succeed in founding a new world in which there will be peace, security and prosperity.

Prime Minister Sjahrir was invited to address the concluding session of the Asian Relations Conference. He expressed the view that "we are living in troubled times and in a world which is very much in a state of flux". The relations among nations might create tensions, but it is incumbent on us to act in such a manner that it becomes palatable to others. In conclusion, he expressed his "warm thanks" to the organizers and to India, in particular, and said: "Many as our faults are, we Indonesians have never been and never will be guilty of ingratitude. Thank you and good bye".

Gandhiji addressed the delegates after Sjahrir spoke. He had returned from Noakhali and Bihar, where there were unprecedented communal clashes. Gandhiji reminded the delegates that the real India was not New Delhi, but its villages. “You can find real India”, Gandhiji added, “in the Bhangi (scavenger) home”. And unless the problems of villages get solved, India would not make any progress. Gandhiji’s speech, in many ways, was in sharp contrast to the general tenor of the Conference, but it made a profound impact on the delegates. For them, seeing Gandhiji in person, “a legend of his time”, was a dream come true.

In his Memoirs, *Tales of a Revolution*, Abu Hanifa has narrated a touching scene. All delegates were eagerly waiting to listen to Gandhiji. He was sitting cross-legged on a small platform. The loudspeaker was too far away. Pandit Nehru stood up from his chair and personally put the microphone near Mahatma Gandhi. He stayed with him as long as the speech lasted. Abu Hanifa whispered to Sjahrir, who was sitting next to him:”That can never happen in Indonesia. Imagine you doing this to Sukarno. Sjahrir just grinned”.

Muslim League Campaign

During the Asian Relations Conference, the representatives of the Muslim League were very active carrying on a pernicious campaign that the Conference was a “Hindu conspiracy” to win international support. The members of the Muslim league naturally got in touch with the Indonesian delegation, for Indonesia, in terms of population, was the largest Muslim country in the world. But the Indonesian delegation was not influenced by this false propaganda. According to Abu Hanifa, the Conference was concerned “with the brotherhood of Asian people and we did not take the so-called Hindu influence in the Conference seriously”.

It was unfortunate that the objective of the Asian Relations Conference, namely, forging friendly relations and promoting co-operation among the people of Asia through a permanent institutional arrangement could not be carried forward. In later years, Asian unity turned out to be a mirage.

In retrospect, we should not under-estimate the significance of the Asian Relations Conference. It heralded the new age of Asian resurgence. As Michael Brecher has pointed out, the Conference reflected "one of the most significant phenomenon of the century, the re-entry of Asia into world politics".

Commemorative Conference

Forty years later, New Delhi organized another Conference to commemorate the fortieth anniversary of the Asian Relations Conference. I was invited to participate in the Conference as a member of the Indian team. There were only two delegates, P.P. Narayanan, well-known trade unionist and Magsaysay award winner, from Malaysia and Madame Siti Wahyunah Sutan Sjahrir from Indonesia. Siti Wahyunah was married to Sjahrir and had accompanied her husband to the Asian Relations Conference. When the two delegates were introduced, there was thunderous applause. Narayanan was given the honour to make his observations in the inaugural session. He went down memory lane and pointed out that India, in 1947, was viewed by nationalists of Asian countries as the "conscience of humanity". He wanted India should play such a role once again.

Madame Siti Wahyunah Sutan Sjahrir, in a paper submitted to the Conference, recalled the turbulent years of Indonesian Revolution. Equally memorable was Prof. Appadorai's message, which was read out by Prof. M. S. Rajan. Appadorai was ailing at that time and could not come to the conference venue. I was an alumnus of the Indian School of International Studies. Prof. Appadorai was the founding Director and, on his retirement, Prof. Rajan had succeeded him. I was deeply moved when Prof. Rajan read out the message sent by Prof. Appadorai.

Moment of Embarrassment

In his Memoirs, Abu Hanifa has written about an embarrassing incident, which took place in Delhi airport when Sjahrir arrived in the capital. Nehru, Indira Gandhi and Abu Hanifa were standing in the front to receive Sjahrir. Sjahrir's first wife, a Dutch woman, named Mies du Chateau, had come from Holland to meet her long-separated husband. She had not seen Sjahrir since he was exiled to West Irian and subsequently to Banda. Mies was keen to give a pleasant shock to Sjahrir. She did not know that Sjahrir had married again and his new bride, Siti Wahyunah, was in the same flight. When the plane landed and Dr. Sjahrir came out with a smile, Mies rushed to greet Sjahrir. The meeting, to quote Abu Hanifa, "was not as warm as expected. We were a little embarrassed, not knowing how Sjahrir would react to the situation". Sjahrir embraced her fleetingly and gave her a peck on both cheeks. The Indonesians were aware that Siti Wahyunah was Sjahrir's favorite wife. To avoid further embarrassment, Sjahrir was immediately put in Nehru's car and the two leaders drove to the city.

❑

8
Together in Struggle

In one of his most inspiring speeches in the mid-night of 14 August, 1947 in the Constituent Assembly, entitled "tryst with destiny" Jawaharlal Nehru said, "At the stroke of the mid-night hour, when the world sleeps, India will awake to life and freedom". Nehru did not take into consideration the time difference between India and the United States. By a strange co-incidence, at the same time, in the United Nations, Nehru's friend and comrade, Dr. Sutan Sjahrir, Prime Minister of the Indonesian Republic, was making a forceful plea for a cease-fire in his country, supervised by an international Commission. The Dutch armed forces should be prevented from snatching a military victory. The innocent people should be saved from bloodshed; and negotiations between Holland and the Republic should commence again.

Nationalist Struggles - Comparative Perspective

A comparison of the ground realities in the two countries should be of great interest. The termination of colonialism in India was not followed by bitterness against the British. Lord Mountbatten, last Viceroy, continued, on Indian request, to be the first Governor General. The Indian Navy was headed by a British Admiral. Jawaharlal Nehru did not want to sever connections with the British completely. As a result, the Republic of India decided to be a member of the Commonwealth.

The immediate consequence was the reconciliation between Winston Churchill and Jawaharlal Nehru. Churchill's Secretary telephoned Jawaharlal Nehru to find out a convenient time so that Churchill could call on the Indian Prime Minister. Nehru replied that he would call on Winston Churchill on his way to the Heathrow airport. Nehru narrated the gist of his conversation with Churchill to his officers while returning to India. Ambassador Jagat Mehta, who accompanied Jawaharlal Nehru as a junior official in the Ministry of External Affairs, has written:

> Churchill, he said, was emotional, almost sentimental and said something to the effect, "Sir, I have done you great wrong. You are like the prodigal who has returned to the fold of the family". The great Churchillian tribute, "Mr. Prime Minister, you have conquered two great human infirmities, you have conquered fear and you have conquered hate" was to come later.

The reconciliation paid rich dividends for both the colonial master and the newly independent country. Britain became the major supplier of arms to independent India. Indian students continued to study in British Universities. And, with the introduction of a welfare state, a number of qualified Indians began to migrate to United Kingdom. Senior officials from the Indian Civil Service (I.C.S.), whom Nehru once characterized as "neither Indian nor civil nor service", continued to serve independent India with great distinction. To illustrate, Sir Girija Shankar Bajpai became the Secretary General of the Ministry of External Affairs. K. P. S. Menon was nominated as the Ambassador to China and, later, to Soviet Union. He retired as Foreign Secretary.

V.P. Menon assisted Sardar Patel in the task of integrating the Indian native States and making India a united country.

Nehru addressed a public meeting in Jakarta during his first visit to independent Indonesia on 6 June 1950. Jawaharlal Nehru highlighted the moral superiority of Gandhian struggle for independence. To quote Nehru:

> The struggle for freedom in India has left no trace of bitterness between peoples of India and Britain. The leaders and people of Indonesia should realize that ultimately it is only through the absence of hatred and through efforts at close co-operation that successful results can be achieved.

The Indonesian experience with Dutch colonialism was different. While Britain saw the writing on the wall and granted independence to India, followed by Burma and Ceylon, Netherlands wanted to re-impose colonialism in East Indies. There was violence and counter violence. When the transfer of power took place in 1949, the Dutch retained West New Guinea. Domestic developments in the two countries took different paths. In Indonesia, the experiment with parliamentary democracy was a failure and led to the introduction of Guided Democracy. Whereas in India, differences between Nehru and Sardar Patel got smoothened, the differences among the Indonesian nationalist triumvirate led to parting of their ways. And finally Sukarno himself was sidelined by the Suharto regime after the traumatic events in 1965.

Exchange of Diplomatic Personnel

Mention has already been made of the functioning of the Indonesian Office in India. Jawaharlal Nehru was very keen to appoint a good diplomat in Jogjakarta, who could interact with the Republican leaders on a day-to-day basis, exchange ideas with them and keep New Delhi posted about fast -changing developments. The Indian Foreign Office faced a dilemma. The Republican control extended to only parts of Java and Sumatra. Rest of the country continued to be under the control of the Dutch. What is more, the Linggadjati Agreement of 1947 was worked out on this basis. How can the representative in Jogjakarta represent Indonesia as a whole? It may not be in conformity with international practices. The issue was resolved by appointing a Consul-General in Batavia and a Consul in Jogjakarta, who would work under the Consul General.

Jawaharlal Nehru chose N. Raghavan to be the Consul General in Batavia. Raghavan was a practising lawyer in Malaya and actively participated in the Indian National Army during the Second World War. Nehru used to correspond with him and also met him during his visit to Malaya and Singapore in 1946. His nationalist credentials were impeccable and Nehru felt that he would devote himself to the betterment of India-Indonesia relations. In a letter dated 8 October 1947, to Raghavan, Nehru instructed him to set up an office in Batavia, and then proceed to Jogjakarta to explain to the nationalist leaders the background as to why India decided to have a Consulate General in Batavia and not in JogJakarta. To quote Nehru:

> You have to tell them that in view of possible International complications we have decided to have a Consulate General in Batavia and not in Jogjakarta. But we propose to have a Consulate in Jogjakata, which will function under the Consulate General. Any other course

> would have simply meant the denial of facilities for our representatives to go to Indonesia or to function there in any other way. Whatever our personal desires might be, a government has to function within certain limitations imposed by international law.

Nehru added that the "whole purpose of sending our representatives is to develop close contacts with the Indonesian Republic and people". In a letter dated 8 October, 1947 to President Sukarno, sent through N. Raghavan, Nehru assured that the main purpose of sending Raghavan and Mohmmad Yunus Khan was "to maintain close contacts with you and your government and to work in co-operation with you".

Introducing Mohammad Yunus to President Sukarno, Nehru wrote that he was a close associate of Khan Abdul Ghaffar Khan (Frontier Gandhi). Nehru added that Yunus "is a dear friend and colleague of mine and I am sure he will make good in Indonesia and you will like him". Mention has already been made earlier to the good work done by Yunus in Jogjakarta. More details will be mentioned later in the chapter.

Dark Clouds over Indonesia

Within few weeks of the signing of the Linggadjati Agreement, the Interim Government extended *de facto* recognition to the Indonesian Republic. The Indian initiative was followed by United Kingdom, United States of America, Australia, China and number of Arab States. The Indian Government also requested the United Nations to admit the Republic of Indonesia in the regional grouping of the Economic Commission of Asia and the Far East

(ECAFE). A meeting of ECAFE was due to be held in New Delhi in 1948.

The Dutch authorities adopted a dogmatic stand on the implementation of the Linggadjati Agreement. Their plan was to set up a "puppet state" in the areas outside Republican control and then use it as a spring board to carry on military operations against the Republic. Their refusal to move with the times and recognize new realities led to a divergence in the interpretation of the Linggadjati Agreement. The Dutch Government resorted to the use of force and unleashed "police action" on the Republican territory on 21 July 1947.

After his return from the Asian Relations Conference, Sjahrir ceased to be the Prime Minister of the Indonesian Republic. He was succeeded by Amir Sharifuddin. However, Sjahrir continued to be close to President Sukarno and became one of his principal advisers. Sukarno instructed Dr. Sjahrir to escape from Indonesia, proceed to New Delhi and mobilize international support for their cause. In an act of heroism and daring, Biju Patnaik rose to the occasion, braved all hazards, avoided the Dutch blockade, flew to Jogjakarta in his Dakota plane and brought Sjahrir to India via Singapore.

Jawaharlal Nehru paid a rich tribute to Biju Patnaik. In a press conference held on 28 July 1947, Nehru said:

> I pay a tribute to the very gallant Indian airman who brought Dr. Sjahrir from Indonesia to New Delhi. He had been known to us for a number of years, not only for his great efficiency in flying, but also for his adventurous and daring spirit… And it is good for India that we should have such young men.

Soon after his arrival in India, Sjahrir declared that he visited India "first" because Nehru was his personal friend and India was the best place to study the international situation and plan the future course of action. Nehru described the sudden attack on the Indonesian Republic as an "astounding thing", which the new "spirit of Asia" would not tolerate. Apart from the merits of the case, Nehru pointed out:

> No European country, whatever it might be, has any business to use its army in Indonesia. Foreign armies functioning in Indonesian soil are an outage to Asian sentiment. The fact that they are bombing a defenceless people is a scandalous thing. If other members of the United Nations tolerate this or remain inactive, then the United Nations Organisation ceases to be.

Nehru pledged every possible help to the Indonesian Republic. On 28 July 1947, Nehru announced that the Dutch Airlines would no longer be allowed to land in India. He requested the dock workers unions not to handle Dutch ships or do anything prejudicial to the interests of the Indonesian Republic. The Indian public opinion was outraged when the Dutch forces shot down an Indian plane carrying Red Cross supplies from Singapore to Jogjakarta. The Interim Government lodged a strong protest with the Dutch Charge *dÕ Affaires*and demanded compensation to the owner, injured and the kith and kin of those killed. In a statement to the press, Nehru characterised the police action as nothing but "well organized war, with bombings of towns on a large scale". The unfortunate situation was that the Indonesian side had no means of defending themselves.

India subscribed to the view that the Dutch aggression was an attempt to undermine not only the Indonesian Republic, but also the United Nations. Just before the United Nations took the Indonesian case for consideration, Nehru declared that "Indonesia has become a symbol and a test for all powers and, more especially, for the United Nations". The Interim Government sent a note to the Secretary General drawing his attention to the situation in Indonesia and requested him to take prompt action for the restoration of peace. Nehru pointed out:

> During the last few days, Dutch forces have embarked without warning on a large scale military action against the Indonesian people. In the opinion of the Government of India, the situation endangers the maintenance of international security, which is covered by Article 30 of the Charter.

During the deliberations in the U.N. Security Council, the Dutch representative objected to the presence of the representative of the Indonesian Republic. The Indian delegate B. R. Sen pointed out that *de facto* recognition had been accorded to the Indonesian Republic by U.K., U.S.A., India, Australia and members of the Arab league, besides Netherlands Government itself. The Indian delegate added:

> It will not be an infringement of International Law if the Security Council extended an invitation to the Republic of Indonesia to attend the meetings of the Security Council.

After two days debate, the Security Council called upon the parties to cease hostilities forthwith and to "settle their dispute by arbitration or by other peaceful means". Complying with the Security Council Resolution, the Dutch and the Republican Governments ordered a cease fire, effective from mid-night 4-5 August 1947. Unfortunately, the Security Council Resolution did not make any mention of withdrawal of the Dutch forces. Even then, the steps taken by the Security Council marked the first victory for India on the Indonesian question.

India and the Struggle for Indonesian Independence

Indian independence, on 15 August 1947, synchronised with the second anniversary of the proclamation of the Indonesian Republic. The Indonesian leaders were convinced that India would spearhead the cause of Indonesian independence. President Sukarno pointed out that much would depend in the near future on India, as to whether the Indonesian people could survive their present crisis and emerge as a really free country. Dr. Sjahrir said, that in moments of great need, "Indonesia has found in India a real friend. We have never been so close to each other at heart before in history".

All India Radio's External Services

New Delhi took a number of significant steps to advance the cause of Indonesian independence. On 12 October 1947, the External Services of the All India Radio started news broadcasts in *Bahasa Indonesia* to disseminate information that would be "without bias and without selfish motive". The *Bahasa Indonesia* programme was the first programme of the External Services. Inaugurating the news service, Sardar Patel said:

> Indonesia is still in the grip of foreign rule and we, who have known the agony

> and anguish of slavery, naturally turn with a feeling of and sympathetic heart to Indonesia in the valiant struggle. India knows that there can be no real freedom so long as there are manacles around Indonesia's wrists.

Medical Assistance to Indonesia

New Delhi stepped up medical assistance to the Indonesian Republic. On 24 August 1947, on an urgent request from the Indonesian Red Cross, the Government of India dispatched a medical mission comprising three doctors, three nurses and three hundred pounds of medical supplies. The medical assistance was gratefully received because the Republic had only one doctor for every 100,000 of its population. The Republican leaders wanted to continue to export rice to India, but their hopes could not be fulfilled due to Dutch obstruction.

De Facto or De Jure Recognition

The Indonesian nationalist leaders were very keen that independent India should accord *de jure* recognition to the Indonesian Republic. They argued that in addition to the unique significance of such a momentous step, the Indian example would be followed by Burma, Pakistan and members of the Arab league. Dr. Soedarsono, Indonesian representative, felt that this step would also strengthen the bargaining position of Indonesia in its negotiations with The Hague. Indonesia appealed to Nehru again, when Mohammad Hatta visited New Delhi. In his Monograph, *Look Up and Aim High*, P. R. S. Mani has mentioned that the "proudest moment" of his life was when he was asked to present Mohmmad Hatta, Vice President of the Republic of Indonesia, to the Secretary General of the Ministry of External affairs. Dr. Hatta handed over a written request for the recognition of the Indonesian Republic.

The Ministry of External Affairs, after carefully weighing the pros and cons, finally decided to continue the prevailing arrangement of *de facto* Recognition. The Indonesian Republic was already receiving "all the facilities that it needs" and *de jure* recognition would not confer any additional advantage. On the contrary, G.S.Bajpai argued, that India's effectiveness to assist Indonesia depended upon the "preservation of a semblance of neutrality".

A few more words about the functioning of the Indian Consulate in Jogjakarta will be in order. The Indian Consulate was the only foreign mission in the Republican capital. Mohammad Yunus had written: "The people could not have been friendlier and the leaders more considerate". During the communist revolt in 1948, the Dutch Government wanted to explain their point of view to Yunus. They took him in a military aircraft, along with the members of the U. N. Good Offices Committee. Yunus was embarassed because Dutch soldiers were dropping leaflets from the aircraft asking the people to surrender. On reaching Jakarta Yunus reported the matter to New Delhi. Yunus had written that the Government of India "lodged a strong protest with the Dutch for having forcefully made our diplomatic representative a participant in the ugly operations against the Indonesians".

A distressing aspect of Indian diplomatic presence in Indonesia needs mention. Factionalism and mud-slinging became the order of the day. Mohammad Yunus, highly self-centred, could not get along with Consul-General N. Raghavan. Yunus had mentioned that Raghavan was "envious and nervous" of him. Ideological differences further widened the chasm between the two Indian diplomats. During the communist revolt in 1948, Raghavan wanted the nationalists to join hands with the Dutch Government and fight the communists together. Yunus knew the nationalist point of view better. However, he was compelled to take up the matter with Sukarno, when Raghavan repeatedly asked him. Sukarno flared up, "I would rather die than use Dutch bullets to kill my people". The differences between the Consul General and the Consul reached ugly levels. Finally, Jawaharlal Nehru recalled Raghavan from Batavia. His successor S. C. Alagappan did not fare better. Nehru warned him, in a letter dated 30 June 1949, not to take sides in the controversies among Indonesian nationalists. Alagappan used to send lengthy notes to New Delhi "almost daily" and used to brag about it. Nehru politely requested Alagappan, "it would have been better if you send somewhat more concise reports". His stay was mercifully short, he was also recalled soon.

Indonesia Mourns Mahatma Gandhi

When the news of Gandhiji's assassination reached Indonesia, the whole country was plunged in grief. Sukarno, with his wife, Padmavati, went to the Indian Consulate and expressed their profound sorrow. Next day, a largely-attended condolence meeting took place. Sukarno spoke with great emotion and referred to Gandhiji as the "pride of Asia and a friend of the downtrodden."

India and Netherlands

Soon after Indian independence, the Government of Netherlands took several initiatives to establish good relations with India. The first initiative was to sign a fresh agreement regarding air services, since the earlier agreement had lapsed. In a letter to Sjahrir, Nehru said that the proposed agreement "will give equal rights to both the parties concerned, that is to say, it will be open to us to have air services on a reciprocal footing". The K.L. M. Airlines was interested to have flights to Batavia from and through India. Jawaharlal Nehru, however, was conscious that the Indonesian nationalists may not favour the Agreement. Therefore, before a final decision was taken, he sought the views of the Republican Government. In a letter to Dr. Sjahrir, dated 15 April 1947, Nehru made the Indian stand very clear. To quote:

> We do not wish to do anything without your approval. As a matter of fact, there is no immediate chance of our developing air services to Indonesia, but the agreement does give us that right and I should like you to confirm it.

In an earlier letter dated 6 April 1947 Nehru had given details. As far as India was concerned, Nehru wrote: "We permit Dutch planes to fly across India. it is entirely a matter between your Government and the Netherlands Government to determine under what conditions Dutch planes should fly over Indonesian territory".

Attempts made by the Government of Netherlands to establish ambassadorial relations with India were also cold shouldered by Jawaharlal Nehru. New Delhi decided not to disturb then existing arrangement where the Indian Ambassador in Paris was also accredited to Netherlands.

❑

9

Indian Diplomacy at Its Best

The main focus of Indian foreign policy in 1948 continued to be Indonesia. In a letter to Mohammad Yunus, dated 18 April 1948, Nehru expressed his desire to have a holiday in Indonesia, meet President Sukarno, whom he had not met so far, and discuss issues of common interest. Nehru underlined that India and Indonesia had to pull together in the future and the two countries should, therefore, start "clearing the ground" and discuss what steps should be taken to promote mutual interest. He was angry with the obstinacy of the Dutch, who continued to be out of touch with political realities. In a letter to the Chief Ministers dated 1 September 1948, referring to Indonesia, Nehru wrote that the "Dutch Government continues to function and to think in the old colonial way". Nehru added that such a policy could "only lead to strife and can never be a solution". Nehru could not visit Indonesia in 1948. He visited Indonesia only in June 1950, after Indonesia attained independence.

India had raised the Indonesian issue in the United Nations in July 1947 and the future of Indonesia continued to be a subject matter of debate in the world body. P. Padmanabha Pillai, Indian delegate, drew the attention of the United Nations to Dutch violations of cease-fire and the need to halt the deteriorating situation:

> To us it is intolerable that after the world has fought two world wars for democracy and national self-determination a colonial war of this kind should be permitted to continue.

Unhappy with the Indian stance, the Dutch delegate tried to unsuccessfully draw a parallel between the colonial war in Indonesia and the communal riots that had taken place in India after partition. Padmanabha Pillai condemned the comparison "as quite gratuitous and irrelevant". After long deliberations, the Security Council appointed a Committee of Good Offices on 25 August 1947, with representatives of Australia, Belgium and the U.S.A., to assist the parties to arrive at a settlement. The Security Council also set up a Consular Commission to supervise the cease-fire order and report on the implementation of the truce. Strangely enough, the Commission consisted of Belgium, France, U.K. and U.S.A. – all Western powers, who could naturally be expected to come to the defence of Holland. The Indian delegate expressed his "profound disappointment" over the strange manner in which the Commission was constituted and pointed out that the Security Council had accepted the "opinion of the accused as to how the trial should be conducted".

Smear Campaign against India

The mounting Indian opposition to the continuance of imperialism in Indonesia, both within and outside the U.N., infuriated the Dutch, who started a smear campaign against India. Van Kleffens, the Dutch delegate in the United Nations, pointed out that in India there was "more military action" than in the "whole of Java and Sumatra put together". A semi-official Dutch document entitled

Indonesia: The Great Powers of Asia and Australia was brought out and widely circulated in Indonesia. Its objective was to project India as a country interested in dominating Asia. To quote from the document:

> India which has for a long time been on the verge of independence and was involved to its advantage in the last war by supplying materials and troops, and then released by England, toys with the idea of Asiatic leadership, which it hopes to assume in succession to Japan. India's history has known expansionism in various directions in Asia and Asia Minor. The present ruling class under the leadership of Pandit Nehru is playing a more modern imperialistic game.

Nobody took these wild and outrageous allegations seriously. D. B. Desai, the Indian delegate, declared in the Security Council that India had no "ulterior motives". He added that no power in Asia "can afford to sit back and look on with equanimity or indifference at the happenings in Indonesia" Throughout 1947, the Dutch Government continued with its acts of aggression in violation of the Security Council's resolutions. Consequently, Republican authority was reduced to Java and Sumatra. The Indonesian nationalists, however, did not lose hope and carried on guerrilla warfare. The U.S., which watched the situation with dismay, did not want an escalation of the conflict and made efforts to bring the two parties together. On U.S. initiative, talks began in the U.S. Naval Ship *Renville* on 8 December 1947. Nehru, naturally, was happy with the American efforts and welcomed the talks. In a message,

Nehru appealed to the two delegations "to work for a similar consummation, in a similar spirit, as the peaceful transfer of power to India from British to Indian hands".

Renville Agreements

The *Renville* Agreements were signed on 17 and 19 January 1948. Sovereignty throughout the Netherlands East Indies was to reside in Holland until the establishment of the United States of Indonesia (U.S.I.). The U.S.I. would be a sovereign and independent state and it will co-exist with the Netherlands in a Union, headed by the Dutch Crown. The status of the Republic was to be that of a constituent state in the United States of Indonesia. Provision was made for internationally supervised plebiscites in Java, Madura and Sumatra to find out whether the people in these states wanted to be a part of the Republic or wanted to be another State in the federal structure. Finally, all the federal units were to be offered "fair representation" in any provisional government. The *Renville Agreements* confirmed the *de facto* truncation of the boundaries of the Republic. Even then, Indonesian nationalists accepted the Agreements because of implicit assurances given by Frank Graham, the U.S. representative in the Good Offices Committee. If the Dutch reneged on the Agreements, the Republican leaders could count on U. S. support. The Government of India's reaction to the Renville Agreements was mixed. It welcomed the Agreements as a step forward towards final settlement. At the same time, New Delhi shared the feelings of the Indonesian nationalists that the Agreements were "arrived at mainly through the concessions which one of the parties had been compelled to make at all stages".

The *Renville* Agreements did not last long. The Dutch resumed their hostile attitude by attempting to establish puppet regimes in Madura and West Java and to block the progress of the Indonesian Republic. The Indian representative drew the attention of the United Nations to the aggressive designs of the Dutch imperialists in total disregard of the Agreements. Describing the Dutch plans as a pre-meditated and carefully worked out strategy, Padmanabha Pillai warned the Security Council that, if such developments were allowed to continue it might lead to the "fragmentation of and dismemberment of the territories of the Indonesian Republic".

Hatta's Incognito Visit to India

The Indonesian leaders were always keen to hold discussions with Jawaharlal Nehru as to the course of action they should follow. Biju Patnaik regularly brought the Indonesian leaders to India. On one occasion Patnaik had arrived in Jogjakarta carrying the much-needed medical

Nehru and Hatta

supplies. After detailed discussions with the Indonesian leaders Patnaik agreed to take Hatta as his co-pilot, named Abdullah. Patnaik arranged for pilot's uniform and also a passport. It took four days for the aircraft to reach New Delhi.

Nehru did not know that Hatta was in India and when Hatta went to Teen *Murti* House, Patnaik informed Nehru that there was a guest from Indonesia called Abdullah, who had a message for him. When Nehru came out and saw Hatta, he was angry with Patnaik. "This is Mohmmad Hatta, why did'nt you tell me his real name?" Patnaik explained why Hatta had come to India in disguise. During the free and frank talks, Hatta asked whether India could provide arms to the Indonesian Republic, because there were definite signs that the Dutch would attack the Republican territory. Nehru responded that matters relating to arms were still with the British Government, so "India could not help in this respect."

Hatta wanted to pay his respects to Mahatma Gandhi and called on him along with Nehru. On being told that the Dutch would attack Indonesian Republic, Gandhiji responded: "I do not believe that Indonesia can be colonized again. The whole world has already condemned colonialism". Nehru told Hatta that the Republic might initially suffer but that would raise the standing of the Republic. Hatta has written in his Memoirs that he agreed with Nehru's view that "a Dutch attack would enhance the international position of the Republic".

Revolt that Failed

In June 1948, the Indonesian Republic had to face not only the Dutch aggressive designs, but also a violent revolt led by the *Partai Kommunis Indonesia* (P.K.I.) or the Indonesian Communist Party. The P. K. I. strategy was partly shaped by the increasing disenchantment with the path of negotiations followed by the Indonesian nationalist leaders and partly by the changing policies of the international communist movement. The revolt in Madium in Java, however, turned out to be a "storm in a tea cup". It was easily put down by the Republican Government, under the capable leadership of General Nasution. The end of the revolt contributed to the immense prestige of Sukarno and the legitimacy of the Republic in the eyes of the world.

Jawaharlal Nehru and the Indian nationalist leaders did not make any specific reference to the communist revolt. At the same time, their sympathies were with the Indonesian nationalists. Faced with a similar threat from the Communist Party of India (C.P.I.), there was nothing surprising about the Indian stance. Nehru was conscious of the threat, which was posed by the communist movements, with powerful ideological support from the Soviet Union and the Chinese Communist Party, to the stability and security of Southeast Asian countries. He was convinced that if the imperialists adopted an intransigent attitude, the nationalist movements would pass on to more revolutionary hands and possibly even to the communists, as it happened in Vietnam and in China. But if freedom was swiftly transferred to non-communist nationalist loaders, the communists could no longer claim to be the spokesmen of nationalist aspirations. The greatest guarantee against communism in Asia, according to Nehru, was the emergence of independent states and establishment of egalitarian societies.

The above analysis is borne out by indirect references contained in the speeches of Jawaharlal Nehru. In a speech in the Constituent Assembly, Nehru said:

> There are all kinds of forces at play in Southeast Asia and, if by misfortune, the forces of progressive nationalism,

> which are represented by the present Government of the Republic of Indonesia does not win, it will be a sad day, not only for Indonesia, but for the rest of Southeast Asia and, may be, even for India.

Benegal Rao was more explicit in his speech in the United Nations on 7 January 1949:

> Our Prime Minister was in no way exaggerating the situation when he said that if no effective measures are taken, the consequences will be disastrous for the whole of Asia and the whole world.

The leaders of the Indonesian Republic were apprehensive that, under the pretext of putting down the communist revolt, the Dutch imperialists would intervene in the affairs of the Republic. But, the United States, during this period, "wisely put strong pressure on the Dutch not to intervene and they were restrained from doing so". The U.S. also exerted pressure on the Netherlands Government to resume negotiations with the Republican leaders. During the talks, the Dutch proposed that, in the Interim Government, the Dutch representative should be vested with the sole authority to employ Netherlands' troops in case of internal disturbances. Hatta rejected it outright. He described the proposals as "indigestible". Compliance with the proposal would have meant signing the death warrant as far as the Republic was concerned. It would not only have infringed on their sovereign rights, but also would have given a convenient pretext for Dutch military intervention.

Second Police Action

The Dutch Government was aware that they were running against time. They wanted to resolve the issue as a *fait accompli* and planned a quick military action. New Delhi was keenly following the developments in Indonesia and apprehended renewed Dutch attack on the Republic. On 4 November 1948, in a meeting in Cairo, Nehru declared that if any further "aggressive action" was taken in Indonesia, it might have "great repercussions in India and the world".

In a bold initiative, Nehru invited Sukarno to come to India, so that he can explain the situation to the international community and also plan the future course of action. On 19 December 1948, Sukarno was awaiting the arrival of the Indian plane, piloted by Biju Patnaik, which was to fly him to India. The Dutch suspected the Indian move, for they feared that Sukarno might escape and set up a provisional government in India. The Dutch, therefore, refused landing facilities in Batavia and also transit facilities in Jogjakarta for the Indian plane. It was obvious that the Dutch wanted to thwart Sukarno's plan for visiting India and timed the police action accordingly. As Prof. Kahin has written, "The timing of the Dutch attack was in part a result of their desire to keep Sukarno from reaching India".

Provisional Government in New Delhi?

The question naturally comes up: What was the Indian response to the request made by the Indonesian nationalists that they would like to establish a Government in exile in New Delhi? According to Iqbal Singh, the author of *Between Two Fires: Towards an Understanding of NehruÕs Foreign Policy*, the idea of getting an aircraft from India was first mooted by Mohmmad Hatta. He asked for the aircraft "to carry away, if necessary, members of the Indonesian Government". Hatta further asked Nehru if India "would allow a provisional Republican Government to function from India in case of need". According to Iqbal Singh,

Nehru mildly demurred to the suggestion and told G. S. Bajpai, the Secretary-General of the Ministry of External Affairs, that it might "lead to serious consequences in regard to our relations with the Dutch". But Nehru was "willing to give shelter to any member of the Indonesian Government". As to what other facilities India could give "will have to be considered later".

Anger and Indignation

The Dutch Government launched the second police action on 19 December 1948. Within a few hours, Jogjakarta, the Republican capital, fell. Leaders of the Republican Government - Sukarno, Hatta and Sjahrir - and the Commander- in-Chief of the Republican Army were detained.

The Dutch military action roused the anger and indignation of the Government and people of India. New Delhi expressed its complete disapproval of the Dutch action and suspended the rights of the Dutch Airlines to fly over India. The departure of Mohan Singh Mehta, Ambassador-designate to Holland, was indefinitely postponed. In a resolution adopted in the Jaipur session of the Indian National Congress, the Congress party extended its full support to the Indonesian people in their struggle for freedom. Addressing the plenary session, Jawaharlal Nehru said:

> I emphasise that no one can prevent the tide of independence in Asian countries. The police action of the Dutch will have serious repercussions in India, in Asia and perhaps in some other countries also.

Indian diplomacy once again asserted itself in the U.N. Security Council. The Security Council held an emergency meeting on the request made by the United States and Australia. Taking part in the debate, D. B. Desai, Indian representative, said that the Indonesian question had become a test for the U.N. Security Council's dignity and self-respect. Pointing out the grave consequences of Dutch military action, Desai declared:

> The struggle of the Indonesian people for freedom epitomizes the spirit that is stirring the whole of Asia. In that continent, there is tremendous upsurge. Every day, events of great consequence are taking place. If this question is not speedily and effectively resolved it will have wide repercussion in that continent.

D.B. Desai, therefore, requested the Security Council to act "immediately and effectively" and order an immediate cease-fire and release of the Indonesian leaders. The Security Council passed a resolution on 24 December 1948, in which it called on all the parties to "cease hostilities forthwith" and asked the Dutch to release the political prisoners immediately. When Holland failed to implement the resolution, the Security Council passed another resolution on 28 December 1948 calling upon Netherlands to set free the political prisoners "forthwith" and to report to the Security Council within the next twenty four hours that it would comply with the U.N. wishes. Netherlands flouted this resolution also. Reacting to the U.N. resolutions, Nehru characterized them as "weak and inadequate".

The Dutch refusal to implement the U.N. resolutions and the Security Council's inability to effectively deal with the Dutch administration disillusioned India. The pro-Dutch stand taken by the Western powers also caused considerable anguish. Nehru declared:

> We have to confess with sorrow that the attitude of some powers in this attempt to destroy the Indonesian Republic has been one of tacit approval of acceptance of aggression.

Crowning Glory – Conference on Indonesia

India's crowning glory in support of Indonesian independence was the Asian Conference on Indonesia held in New Delhi from January 20-23, 1949. Nehru was seriously thinking of the steps to be taken in support of the Indonesian Republic in the new situation created by the Dutch military action and the inability of the U.N. Security Council to respond positively to Indonesian aspirations. Nehru declared on the very day the Dutch launched the military action: "We will have to re-consider what we may have to do under the circumstances". Nehru got in touch with other Asian leaders; U Nu, the Burmese leader, suggested the convening of an international conference. Nehru concurred and decided to convene an Asian Conference in New Delhi.

The Indian initiative evoked mixed reactions. The Republican Government was naturally elated and hailed the proposed conference on Indonesia as the "most encouraging manifestation of international concern". As was to be expected, the Dutch authorities were very angry and expressed concern over Nehru's action in calling a conference "to discuss the internal affairs of another country". The United States had its reservations and asked New Delhi not to adopt extreme postures which would lead to a "breach of relations with Holland".

From the very beginning, Nehru took care to allay the fears of Western countries regarding the objectives of the

Conference. Addressing the Indian Journalists Association in Calcutta, he stated categorically that it was not India's intention to form an "Asian bloc" against European countries or America. The Conference "is not opposed to any country or people. It is not anti-European or anti-American or anti-Western". The External Affairs Ministry explained that the purpose of the Conference was to "reinforce the United Nations, not to replace it". The Conference was intended to make the Security Council realize the strong feelings in Asia on the subject of imperialist aggression. Nehru himself made this point clear in his invitation letter to various countries. "The Conference is not designed to supersede in any way the activities of the Security Council, but only to lend the Council support on the basis of understanding among ourselves".

The Asian Conference on Indonesia assembled in New Delhi on 20 January, 1949. Since the objective was to assist Indonesia attain its freedom, only those countries which supported the Indonesian cause were invited. They included Afghanistan, Australia, Burma, Ceylon, Egypt, Ethiopia, India, Iran, Iraq, Lebanon, Pakistan, the Philippines, Saudi Arabia, Syria and Yemen. China, Nepal, Thailand and New Zealand were represented by observers. Leading members of either bloc were excluded and the membership of the Conference was limited to those which were "either neighboring or directly involved". India did not want the Indonesian question to be embroiled in any controversy.

Inaugurating the eighteen- nation Conference, Nehru declared:

> We meet today because the freedom of a sister country of ours has been

> imperiled and the dying colonialism of a past age has raised its head again and challenged all the forces that are struggling to build a new structure in the world. That challenge has a deeper significance than might appear on the surface, for it is a challenge to a newly awakened Asia which has so long suffered under various forms of colonialism.

Nehru reiterated that the Conference was meeting "in no spirit of hostility to any nation or any grouping". He also emphasized that the Conference was not intended to bypass the United Nations, but to help the Security Council to bring about a rapid and peaceful solution to the Indonesian problem. To quote Nehru: "We meet to supplement the efforts of the Security Council, not to supplant that body". Nehru cautioned that if the Dutch challenge was not met effectively, "it would affect not merely Indonesia, but also Asia and the entire world".

Nehru urged the Conference to devote attention to three subjects, namely, 1) To frame and submit proposals to the Security Council for the immediate restoration of peace and early realization of the freedom of the Indonesian people; 2) To suggest to the Security Council what action should be taken in case its recommendations were not carried and 3) To devise machinery and procedure to meet threat to freedom of Asian countries.

In a Memorandum submitted to the Conference, the Indonesian nationalists urged the inclusion of their proposals in the final memorandum to be submitted to the United Nations. Their proposals included the formation of an Interim Government by 1 March 1949; holding the general elections to a Constituent Assembly by 1 July 1949; transfer of complete sovereignty by 1 December 1949; applying the provisions of Articles 41 and 42 of the U.N. Charter if the Dutch failed to carry out its recommendations; and extending *de jure* recognition to the Republican Government before the establishment of an Interim Government.

The Conference, after three days of free and frank discussions, unanimously adopted three resolutions. The first resolution declared that the Dutch military action against the Indonesian Republic constituted a "flagrant violation of the Charter of the United Nations and defiance of the efforts of the Security Council and Its Good Offices Committee to bring about a peaceful solution". The Conference recommended to the Security Council that all Republican leaders be freed immediately and the freedom of the Republican Government be restored; an Interim Government to be formed before 15 March 1949; and power over the whole of Indonesia be completely transferred by 1 January 1950 to the United States of Indonesia. It also suggested that the Security Council take effective action, under the wide powers conferred upon by the Charter "in case its recommendations were not complied with". Finally, the Conference requested the Security Council to report to the General Assembly the progress made in solving the Indonesian issue.

The Conference activated the Security Council and the international community took greater interest in Indonesia. The U.N. Security Council adopted a Resolution on 28 January 1949, which incorporated the spirit and words of the resolutions passed by the Conference on Indonesia. However, in the time table for the transfer of power, the Security Council made one important change by fixing 1 July 1950 as the deadline for the termination of sovereignty, instead of 1 January 1950.

India and Indonesia were not completely happy with the U.N. Resolutions. At the same time, they were also not completely dissatisfied, because, for the first time, the Security Council had laid down terms for a definitive political settlement of the Indonesian problem. The Resolution also, as Prof. Alastair Taylor has argued, put the Indonesian Republic "in a stronger position", because it asked the Government of Netherlands to re-commence negotiations with the Republican Government. For, according to The Hague, the Republican Government "had ceased to exist".

Resumption of Negotiations

Negotiations began between the Government of Netherlands and Indonesian nationalists in November 1949. Netherlands agreed to the complete and unconditional transfer of sovereignty before 30 December 1949 of the entire territory of the former East Indies, except the West New Guinea, to the Republic of the United States of Indonesia (R.U.S.I.), a federal Government comprising of the Republic of Indonesia and the fifteen political units established by the Dutch. The only problem that remained unresolved was the status of West New Guinea. However, a compromise formula was evolved according to which the control and administration of Netherlands was to continue in West New Guinea till its political status "was determined through negotiations" between Netherlands and the R.U.S.I. within a year from the date of transfer to the R.U.S.I.

Thus came to an end another colonial empire in the most populous country in Southeast Asia. Jawaharlal Nehru proudly declared that the birth of the United States of Indonesia "marked the beginning of a new leaf in the history of Asia".

Request for Military Aid

Since the declaration of independence on 17 August 1945, Indonesian leaders have repeatedly requested for military aid from India Jawaharlal Nehru adopted a cautious approach and, as mentioned earlier, he told Mohammad Hatta that it would not be possible to provide military aid. But the Republican leaders did not lose hope. They repeated the request when it was known that India, along with Commonwealth countries, was providing military aid to Burma to buttress the U Nu regime. Had it not been for Commonwealth assistance, the U Nu government would have perhaps lost the battle for survival. Both India and Britain provided Burma with 10,000 small weapons each and arranged with other Commonwealth countries, including Australia, Ceylon and Pakistan, to provide a loan of six million pounds sterling to tide over the economic crisis.

It must, however, be pointed out that there were basic differences between the Burmese and Indonesian situations. Burma was an independent country, struggling against domestic rebels, whereas Indonesia was a classic case of nationalists fighting against the imperialists. International assistance was provided to Burma on the specific request made by a legitimate government of the country. Nehru was deeply sensitive of these basic differences. In a note on "India and Indonesia", penned by Jawaharlal Nehru on 28 June 1949, Nehru explained the "underlying principles governing the relations between the two countries".

Nehru pointed out that over the years, a "close bond between India and Indonesia" and a "sense of intimacy" had developed between the two countries. The continuation of Dutch rule in Indonesia was dangerous from many points of view and would be a "source of perpetual trouble and conflict in Southeast Asia". The only way to provide stability and security to the region is for Indonesia to become free and function in an independent manner. During the critical phase of Indonesian struggle for independence "India had been of some service … that service we will continue to render … because it is in consonance with our basic policy".

According to Jawaharlal Nehru, "occasionally demands have reached us for some kind of military assistance" either in the shape "of arms and ammunition or even more active help". Nehru wanted to make the "position clear" and explained that India had practically exhausted the surplus military stores it had in the military operations in Kashmir and was sending missions to Europe and America to get military equipments. Apart from this practical problem, Nehru explained another significant dimension of the issue. Even if India wanted to extend military help to Indonesia, "it cannot do so without facing the Dutch blockade". Any attempt to militarily help Indonesia would lead to a war with the Netherlands, which would not be of any help to Indonesia. Moreover, it would be a "defiance of the United Nations". Therefore, Nehru ruled out any military assistance to Indonesia at the official level.

It must be added that on a specific request made by Sjahrir, facilities were made available for the training of Indonesian pilots by private agencies in Allahabad. The Indonesian army was not well equipped at the time of independence and, therefore, it was essential to expand training facilities. Naturally, Sjahrir's attention turned to India. A batch of 18 young men was sent to Hind Provincial Flying Club in Bamrauli, Allahabad. These cadets later rose to high positions in Indonesian Air Force, and were known as *Angkataan Panerbang India* – India Pilot Branch. After the training in Allahabad, they could not immediately go back to Indonesia, so they proceeded to Burma and assisted the U Nu government in their fight against the Kachins and the Karens.

Differences among Indonesian Nationalists

Jawaharlal Nehru was deeply pained and distressed that, instead of presenting a united front against the Dutch colonialists, the Indonesian nationalists were fighting among themselves. As a matter of principle, Jawaharlal Nehru never interfered in the domestic politics of other countries. But since Nehru's relations with Sukarno, Hattta and Sjahrir were on "intimate terms", he wrote and appealed to them to sink their differences in a spirit of amity and good will for the all round development of Indonesia. In a letter dated 30 June 1949 to President Sukarno, Jawaharlal Nehru wrote:

> If I may venture to offer one piece of advice of a rather general kind it is that nothing is more important for a national movement than to keep closely knit together and to present a common and united front against the enemy. Whether in India or Indonesia or elsewhere, our opponents have always tried to split the unity of the national movement and then to take advantage of the ensuing weakness and confusion of mind.

In a letter to Mohammed Hatta, Nehru pointed out:

> I have faith that the cause of the Indonesian Republic will triumph.

> My only apprehension is that in the prolonged negotiations and maneuvers of the Dutch, doubt and confusion may arise in the minds of the leaders of the Republic, leading to a loosening of the close bonds that hold them together. That would be more unfortunate than any other development can be.

The letter to Sjahrir echoed the same sentiments:

> You will forgive me if I write about a matter which has troubled me somewhat. I am greatly concerned about the differences of opinion among the leaders of the Republic are growing. Differences there must be, but it seems to me of the first importance that the leaders of the Republic should hold together and jointly face the enemy. A wrong step may be righted and an error corrected, but if there are internal dissensions that means an inner weakness which is bound to do injury to the cause.

The greatest tragedy of Indonesia after independence was the lack of unity among those who built up the national movement, brick by brick, against heavy odds. And the country had to pay a heavy price for this default.

Conclusion

The independence of Indonesia was not only a great event in Indonesian history, but it was also a landmark in India-Indonesia relations. The Government of India was represented by Dr. Rajkumari Amrit Kaur in the transfer of power ceremony. In a press conference in Jakarta, she said that perhaps no other country in the world "rejoiced more sincerely than India" at the advent of Indonesian independence, because "right from the beginning", India had been a comrade in struggle.

Throughout India, there was great joy and fervour on the day of Indonesian independence. Speaking on the occasion of the flag hoisting ceremony at the official residence of the Indonesian representative, Jawaharlal Nehru declared:

> Today the brave and loveable people of Indonesia, after great turmoil, are emerging as an independent sovereign people…It is really a historic moment for Asia. For today, it is not merely Indonesia, but the great continent of Asia which is gradually coming into its own.

The mutual affection and love, which bound India and Indonesia together, was eloquently echoed by Dr. Soedarsono, the Indonesian representative, in India:

> We want the Prime Minister of India to accept the heartfelt gratitude and thanks of millions of Indonesians, unknown to him, but whose cause he has championed so eloquently, for the numerous acts of help, for the kind, friendly, and wise advice and hospitality he has given to all our leaders and the Government of the Republic of Indonesia.

❑

10

Bliss was it in that Dawn to be Alive

I would like to conclude the book with a snap shot of one of the memorable events in India-Indonesia relations. It took place on 27 January 1950 in Delhi University. On a request made by Jawaharlal Nehru, the Delhi University decided to confer an honorary doctorate on President Sukarno. The earlier day, Sukarno, accompanied by his wife Padmavati, was the chief guest in the first Republic Day parade. As Sukarno and Padmavati arrived in *Rajpath*, accompanied by Rashtrapati Rajendra Prasad, there was wild jubilation and cheer from the assembled crowd.

While perusing the historical records, I was able to get some valuable information on the background to Sukarno's visit to India. The Indonesian nationalists were very keen that Nehru should be present at the time of transfer of power from Holland to Indonesia on 27 December 1949. Nehru was extremely busy and could not go to Indonesia at that time. He deputed Dr. Rajkumari Amrit Kaur to represent India. India was also keen to establish full diplomatic relations between the two countries. Dr. Subbarayan was appointed as the first Indian Ambassador to Indonesia. Soon after arriving in Jakarta, Subbarayan, accompanied by Rajkumari Amrit Kaur, called on President Sukarno. In a letter to Jawaharlal Nehru, Dr. Subbarayan has mentioned that in the course of their informal talks, Sukarno expressed his desire to be present at the first Republic Day on 26 January 1950. New Delhi was very happy to extend the invitation and President Sukarno, with his wife, Padmavati, came to India.

In the Delhi University convocation, the roles were reversed. Jawaharlal Nehru, as is well known, used to conclude his speech with Jai Hind. Jai Hind used to be repeated three times, each time Nehru exhorting the crowd louder, louder. In the convocation, it was Sukarno who said Jai Hind three times. Nehru did not lag behind. He ended his speech by saying *Merdeka* three times. *Merdeka* means freedom in Bahasa Indonesia. During the freedom struggle, the archipelago used to resonate with the slogan *Merdeka.*

Students of Delhi University requested Sukarno to speak in English language. Sukarno referred to the request in the beginning of his speech and said that he wanted to speak in Hindustani, but he did not know the language. Then he turned to Maulana Azad, Education Minister, and requested him to send some teachers to Indonesia who could teach Hindustani to the students. In his speech, Nehru referred to India's age old cultural contacts with Indonesia and how *Bahasa Indonesia was* full of Sanskrit words. He referred, in particular, to Sukarno's name, how Sukarno's father changed his name from Kusno to Karno, after the great hero of Mahabharata. Nehru also referred to Sukarno's wife Padmavati and their daughter Meghawati Satyavati Sukarno Putri.

To the assembled students of Delhi University, it was a memorable day. They were meeting in person two of Asia's greatest nationalist leaders. A seasoned speaker, Sukarno held the students in the hollow of his palm. He could say the right things at the right time in the right manner. My friend, P.B. Venkatasubramanyam, was a student in the law faculty at that time. Reminiscing about the convocation, he quoted the famous lines of Wordsworth on French Revolution: "Bliss was it in that dawn to be alive, but to have been young was very heaven". Venkatasubramanyam retired from the Government of India as Law Secretary and settled down in Chennai.

The same evening, Sukarno attended an "At Home" organized by the Indian Council of World Affairs in the Constitution Club. Pandit Hridaynath Kunzru presided. Sukarno allowed his poetic imagination to explain India's abiding cultural influences in Indonesia and how, in later years, the nationalist leaders developed bonds of respect and affection. He quoted from a poem included in the presidential speech of Sarojini Naidu, delivered three years earlier, in the Asian Relations Conference. To quote: "Come to my country, Come to the Mother. The doors of this house are always open. It has a roof of snow peaks, its doors are two oceans. Come to the Mother".

Ambassador P. R. S. Mani narrated an incident which is worth repetition. From New Delhi Sukarno and Padmavati went to Karachi, then capital of Pakistan. The Pakistani media could not reconcile to the fact that a Moslem woman could have a Hindu name. One Pakistani newspaper had the headlines:"Sukarno, with his wife Fatima, is coming to Pakistan today".

In the later part of his life, Sukarno was defamed and denigrated by the Western media as well as by his political opponents in Indonesia. His yeoman contributions to the freedom of his country and to nation building were downplayed and downgraded. And when his tragic end came on Sunday, 21 June 1970, his wives Hartini and Dewi begged Suharto to have him buried in the garden of his *Batu*

Tulis home. Sukarno himself had chosen that place for final rest, because he believed that the nearby stone had mystical powers. But Suharto and his colleagues did not want a place of pilgrimage very near Jakarta. On Monday, 22 June 1970, Sukarno was buried next to his mother at Biltar. As the crow flies, Biltar is 623 kms away from Jakarta. The end result is there is no monument in Jakarta, like Raj Ghat, in New Delhi, so that those who love Indonesia can pay their respects to the Father of the Nation.

As a student of history, committed to foster and promote India-Indonesia relations, how will I remember Sukarno? "Bung Karno, you will ever remain green in my memory. For me you are like Gandhiji, Jawaharlal Nehru and Ho Chih Minh".

❑

BIBLIOGRAPHY

PRIMARY SOURCES

1. Central Legislative Assembly Debates
2. Constituent Assembly Debates
3. Gopal, S, Ed., Selected *Works of Jawaharlal Nehru*, 1927-1950
4. *Collected Works of Mahatma Gandhi*
5. Nehru Memorial Museum and Library, *Oral History* Project
6. National Archives, *Indonesia Papers*
7. *Asian Relations* (New Delhi, 1948)
8. Gonsalves, Eric, Ed., *Asian Relations* (New Delhi, 1991)
9. United Nations, General Assembly, Official Records
10. United Nations, Security Council, Official Records

BOOKS

1. Abu Hanifa, *Tales of A Revolution* (Singapore, 1972)
2. All India Congress Committee, *A Centenary History of the Indian National Congress, Vol. III* (New Delhi, 1985)
3. Anderson, B., *Java in the Time of Revolution* (Ithaca,1972)
4. Baig, M.R.A., *In Different Saddles* (Bombay, 1967)
5. Brecher, Michael, "*NehruÕs Place in Histor*ỷ, Israel, Milton, Ed., *Nehru and the Twentieth Century* (Toronto, 1991)

6. Damodaran A.K., *Beyond Autonomy: Roots of IndiaÕs Foreign Policy*(New Delhi, 2000)
7. Das M.N., *The Political Philospphy of Jawaharlal Nehru* (London, 1960)
8. Das Gupta, Arun, "India-Indonesia Relations: The Search for A New Perspective", Gonsalves Eric, Ed., *Asian Relations* (New Delhi, 1991)
9. Das Gupta, Arun, "Intellectual and Academic Co-operation between India and Southeast Asia", Ghoshal Baladas, Ed., *India and Southeast Asia: Challenges and Opportunities* (New Delhi, 1996)
10. Das Gupta, Shakti, *TagoreÕs Asian Outlook* (Calcutta, 1981)
11. Dham, Bernard, *Sukarno and the Struggle for Indonesian Independence* (Ithaca, 1966)
12. Dharma Kumar, Ed., *Comparative History of India and Holland, Volume IV* (Leiden, 1989)
13. Dorling Philip and Lee David, *Documents on Australian Foreign Policy, 1937-1949, Vol. XIII, Indonesia 1949* (Canberra, n.d.)
14. Dutt, Subimal, *With* (Calcutta, 1977)
15. Emerson, Rupert, *From Empire to Nation: The Rise and Self-Assertion of Asian and African Peoples* (Cambridge, Massachusetts, 1962)
16. Engineer, Asghar Ali, *A Living Faith* (New Delhi, 2011)
17. Feith, Herbert, Ed., *Indonesian Political Thinking 1946-1965* (Ithaca, 1970)
18. Fischer, Louis, *The Story of Indonesia* (New York, 1959)
19. Geertz, Clifford, *Religion of Java* (Chicago, 1976)
20. Ghoshal, Baladas, Ed., *India and Southeast Asia: Challenges and Opportunities* (New Delhi, 1996)

21. Gopal, S, *Jawaharlal Nehru, A Biography (New Delhi, 1979)*
22. Government of Indonesia, *Illustrations of the Revolution, 1945-1950 (Jakarta, 1954)*
23. Idi Anak Agung Gde Agung, *Twenty Years of Indonesian Foreign Policy, 1945-1965 (The Hague, 1973)*
24. Israel, Milton, Ed., *Nehru and the Twentieth Century* (Toronto, 1991)
25. James, Rush, "Anticipating An Asian Century", Ramachandra Guha, Ed., *Makers of Modern Asia (New Delhi, 2014)*
26. Jha, C.S., *From Bandung to Tashkent: Glimpses of IndiaÕs Foreign Policy*(Madras, 1983)
27. Kahin, George McTurnan, *Nationalism and Revolution in Indonesia* (Ithaca, 1962)
28. Kahin, George McT, *Southeast Asia: A Testament* (London, 2013)
29. Khoo Kay Hock, *The Development of Indonesian Nationalism* (Singapore, n.d.)
30. Karunakaran, K.P., *India in World Affairs*, August 1947 – January 1950 (Bombay, 1952)
31. Khanolkar, G.F., *The Lute and the Plough: A Life of Rabindranath Tagore* (Bombay, 1954)
32. Kripalani, Krishna, *Rabindranath Tagore: A Biography* (London, 1962)
33. Leifer, Michael, *IndonesiaÕs Foreign Policy* (London, 1983)
34. Leifer, Michael, "The Changing Temper of Indonesian Nationalism", Michael Leifer, Ed., *Asian Nationalism* (London, 2000)
35. Legge, J.D., *Sukarno: A Political Biography* (Sydney, 1972)

36. Legge, J.D., *Indonesia, Second edition* (Sydney, 1977)

37. Levi, Werner, *Free India in Asia* (Minneapolis, 1952)

38. May, Reginald, *The Culture of South-East Asia* (New Delhi, 1962)

39. McMahon, Robert J, *Colonialism and Cold War: The United States and The Struggle for Indonesian Independence* (Ithaca, 1981)

40. Majumdar, R.C., *Hindu Colonies in the Far East (Calcutta, 1963)*

41. Majumdar, R.C., *Ancient Indian Colonisation in Southeast Asia* (Baroda, 1963)

42. Majumdar, R.C., *India and Southeast Asia* (New Delhi, 1979)

43. Mani, P.R.S., *The Story of Indonesian Revolution, 1945 -1950*, (University of Madras, 1986)

44. Mani, P.R.S., *Jelak Revolusi* 1945: *sebuah kesaksian sejarah* (Jakarta, 1989)

45. Mani, P.R.S., *Look Up and Aim High* (Chennai, 2005)

46. McVey, Ruth T., Ed., *Indonesia*, (New Haven, 1963)

47. Mehta, Jagat Singh, "The Nehru We loved to Serve" (A Personal Nostalgia), Israel Milton, *Nehru and the Twentieth Century* (Toronto, 1991)

48. Mehrish, Brijesh Narain, *IndiaÕs Recognition Policy Towards the New Nations* (Delhi, 1972)

49. Misra, K.P., Ed. *Foreign Policy of India: A Book of Readings* (New Delhi, 1977)

50. Nanda, B.R., *IndiaÕs Foreign Policy: The Nehru Years* (New Delhi, 1976)

51. Nehru, Jawaharlal, *The Discovery of India* (London, 1946)

52. Nilakanta Sastri, K.A., *South Indian Influences in the Far East (Bombay, 1949)*
53. Nilakanta Sastri, K.A., *History of Sri Vijaya* (Madras, 1949)
54. Paget, Robert K, Ed., *Indonesia Accuses: SukarnoÕs Defence Oration in the Political Trial* of 1930 (Melbourne, 1975)
55. Penders, C.L.M., Ed., *Mohammad Hatta: Indonesian Patriot: Memoirs* (Singapore, 1981)
56. Penders, C.L. M., *The Life and Times of Sukarno* (London, 1974)
57. Poplai, S.L, Ed., *India, 1947-1950, Vol. 2, External Affairs* (London, 1969)
58. Prasad, Bimla, *The Origins of Indian Foreign Policy*, (Calcutta, 1962)
59. Prasad, Birendra, *Indian Nationalism and Asia* (Delhi, 1979)
60. Ray, Jayanta Kumar, *Transfer of Power in Indonesia* (Bombay, 1967)
61. Reddy, E. S. and Damodaran, A.K., *Decolonisation, Peace and the United Nations: Krishna MenonÕs Speeches in the United Nations* (New Delhi, 1997)
62. Reid, A.J.S., *IndonesiaÕs National Revolution, 1945-1950* (Victoria, 1970)
63. Saran, Malini and Khanna, Vinod, *The Ramayana in Indonesia* (New Delhi, 2004)
64. Sen, B.R., *Towards A Newer World* (Dublin, 1982)
65. Shanmugam, S.V., *Indonesian Studies* (New Delhi, 1979)
66. Singh, Iqbal, *Between Two Fires: Towards An Understanding of Jawaharlal NehruÕs Foreign Policy, Volume 1 and 2* (Nehru Memorial Museum and Library, New Delhi)

67. Sharma, Navrekha and Ghoshal, Baladas, *IndiaÕs Relations with Indonesia* (Singapore, 2014)
68. Sjahrir, Sutan, *Our Struggle* (Translated by Benedict Anderson) (New York, 1968)
69. Soekarno, *Under the Banner of Revolution* (Jakarta,1966)
70. Sukarno, *An Autobiography as Told to Cindy Adams (Hong Kong,* 1966)
71. Suryanarayan, *V., India and the Indonesian Revolution* (Presidential address delivered in Section IV – Countries other than India - of the forty second session of the Indian History Congress held in Magadh University, Bodh Gaya), 28 December 1981.
72. Suryanarayan, V. "Evolution of Nehru's Thinking on Foreign Policy", C.N. Somarajan, Ed., *Formulation and Practice of IndiaÕs Foreign Policy* (New Delhi, 1993)
73. Suryanarayan, V, "Looking Ahead: India and Southeast Asia in the 1990's: New Perspectives, New Challenges", Ghoshal, Baladas Ed., *India and Southeast Asia: Challenges and Opportunities* (New Delhi, 1996)
74. Suryanarayan,V., *India and Southeast Asia: Search for Substance* (Presidential Address, Southeast Asia Section, Indian Congress of Asian and Pacific Studies, Hyderabad, 1996)
75. Taufik, Abdullah, Ed., The *Heartbeat of Indonesian Revolution* (Jakarta, 1995)
76. Taylor, M. Alastair, *Indonesian Independence and the United Nations* (Connecticut, 1960)
77. Ton That Thien, *India and Southeast Asia* (Geneva, 1963)

78. Tyabji, Badr-ud-din, *Memoirs of An Egotist* (New Delhi, n.d.)
79. Wilson, Greta O, Edited and Translated, *Regents, Reformers, and Revolutionaries: Indonesian Voices of Colonial Days, Selected Historical Readings, 1899-1949* (Hawaii, 1978)
80. Van Leur, *Indonesian Trade and Society: Essays in Asian Social and Economic History* (The Hague, 1967)
81. Woodman, Dorothy, *The Republic of Indonesia* (London, 1956)
82. Yunus, Mohammad, *Persons, Passions and Politics* (New Delhi, 1979)

Newspapers and Journals

1. *The Hindu (Madras),* 1945-1950
2. *India Quarterly (New Delhi)*
3. Indonesia Quarterly (Jakarta)
4. Indonesia (Ithaca)

Unpublished Materials

1. Lakshmana Chetty, A, *IndiaÕs Policy in Southeast Asia, 1947-1954* (Dissertation submitted for the award of the Degree of Doctor of Philosophy, University of Madras)
2. Suryanarayan V., *Glimpses into Golden Era of India- Indonesia Relations* (Paper submitted in the International Seminar on Kalinga-Indonesia Dialogue, November 14-16, 2016)
3. Suryanarayan V. *ÒIndiaÕs Policy towards Southeast Asia: A Critical AppraisalÓ* Valedictory Address delivered in the International Conference on "India-ASEAN: Towards Greater Partnership"

organized by the Centre for Southeast Asian and Pacific Studies, Sri Venkateswara University, iirupati, 4-5 December 2017

Articles from the Internet

1. Bose, Sugata, "*Rabindranath* 'Tagore and Asian Universalism"' (Singapore, 2010) *Institute of Southeast Asian Studies (ISEAS), https://www.iseas.edu.sg/images/centres/nalanda_sriwijaya_centre/nsc_tagore_booklet_small.pdf*
2. Heather, Goddall, 'Writing Conflicted Loyalties: An Indian Journalist's Perspectives on the Dilemmas of Indian Troops in Indonesia", *Warinasia, http://www.warinasia.com/heather-goodall-part-2/*
3. Das Gupta, Arun,, "Rabindranath Tagore in Indonesia: An Experiment in Bridge Building", (Leiden, 20020, *KITLV, http://booksandjournals.brillonline.com docserver/22134379/158/3/22134379_158_03_s03 text.*

❑

INDEX

B

C

D

E

F

G

H

❑❑❑